SEW...

The Garment–Making Book of Knowledge

Real-Life Lessons from a Serial Sewist

Barbara Emodi

stash BOOKS

an imprint of C&T Publishing

Text copyright © 2018 by Barbara Emodi

Photography and artwork copyright © 2018 by C&T Publishing, Inc.

PUBLISHER: Amy Marson

CREATIVE DIRECTOR: Gailen Runge

EDITOR: Karla Menaugh

TECHNICAL EDITOR: Debbie Rodgers

COVER/BOOK DESIGNER: April Mostek

PRODUCTION COORDINATOR: Zinnia Heinzmann

PRODUCTION EDITOR: Alice Mace Nakanishi

ILLUSTRATORS: Kirstie L. Pettersen and Leo Booth

PHOTO ASSISTANT: Mai Yong Vang

COVER PHOTOGRAPHY by Lucy Glover and Mai Yong Vang of C&T Publishing, Inc.,

STYLE PHOTOGRAPHY by Lucy Glover and
INSTRUCTIONAL PHOTOGRAPHY by Mai Yong Vang of C&T Publishing, Inc., unless otherwise noted

Published by Stash Books, an imprint of
C&T Publishing, Inc., P.O. Box 1456, Lafayette, CA 94549

Library of Congress Cataloging-in-Publication Data

Names: Emodi, Barbara, 1953- author.

Title: Sew ... the garment-making book of knowledge :
real-life lessons from a serial sewist / Barbara Emodi.

Description: Lafayette, CA : C&T Publishing, Inc., 2018. |
Includes bibliographical references.

Identifiers: LCCN 2017045270 | ISBN 9781617456046
(soft cover)

Subjects: LCSH: Machine sewing.

Classification: LCC TT713 .E46 2018 |
DDC 646.2/044--dc23

LC record available at https://lccn.loc.gov/2017045270

Printed in China

10 9 8 7 6 5 4 3 2

Dedication

In memory of the Sew 'n' Sews, my grandmother's sewing group for 65 years in Winnipeg, and for my creative grandchildren—Scarlett, Heidi, and Billy—who will take all this much further.

Acknowledgments

First I have to thank my mother, who taught me to sew. You were the only mother in town to send a twelve-year-old off to take adult sewing classes. Still not sure what a kid that age was supposed to do with a fully lined wool suit, but I do know the skills I learned then I still use today.

My love and appreciation, too, to my most wonderful children. Thank you, Katrina, for wearing every one of my experiments to school without complaining and for the pen you gave me once long ago "to my mother the writer." Thank you, Nat, for being my consigliere in life and all projects and for sharing my love of fine fabrics and construction. And to my youngest, Ben, who once shouted to me from the sandbox, "I don't want to go to shopping, Mom, just take my measurements," thank you for summing up the house you all grew up in.

Hugs as well to my infinitely patient and kind husband, Leo, who did the technical drawings in Chapter 5. No one will ever know how much you did to make this book happen, but I do.

My sewing buddies, Trudy Winfield and the late Sue Mowat Perry; **my friends at the Atlantic Sewing Guild** in Halifax, Nova Scotia; and **my many sewing students** over the years—you all have taught me so much about good sewing and good company.

Thanks to Martin Favre and Adrienne Gallagher of BERNINA, who made it possible for me to work with a machine that was frequently smarter than I am—the BERNINA 740—and made sewing the samples and garments pictured throughout the book nothing but a pleasure.

Special thanks, too, to the talented designers who have continued to produce amazing sewing patterns—Jeanne and Émilie at Jalie Patterns, Louise Cutting of Cutting Line Designs, and Chloe and her team at Style Arc, among many others

Finally, a special mention for my small black rescue dog who sat pressed to my hip while I sewed every sample and wrote every word. It's done now, Daisy, good girl … let's go get the leash!

Contents

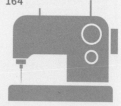

Introduction:
For Sewists
Like You

I decided to write this book the day I realized how lucky I was. I was reading the sewing blogs of some fabulous young sewists when it hit me—my people are back.

Interest in sewing has skipped at least one generation, but sewing, my culture, is experiencing a resurgence.

I am thrilled about this. I feel lucky to be part of this energy. At the same time, I also feel lucky to have had access in my own life to so much fundamental sewing knowledge, almost as a birthright.

So much of what I know about sewing was passed down to me. My mother, never in love with things domestic, still made sure I knew about grain, how to make a tailor tack, and why the inside should always look as good as the outside. She learned these things from her own mother, who had learned them during an apprenticeship with an Edinburgh tailor.

I also grew up in a time when all the big stores had fabric departments and when newspapers sold good mail-order patterns. I grew up when home economics was a serious profession for serious women and when girls made their graduation dresses and even their wedding gowns. I grew up in a time when every house had a sewing machine.

However, at some point the sewing crowd around me thinned out. Friends started to ask me to sew for them, rather than with them. I am not sure where all the sewists went. When women were no longer expected to sew, many of them didn't.

So those of us who started to sew as children and never stopped have in our own way become sort of sewing cultural repositories. In our heads are all the things our mothers and grandmothers taught us, all the information we acquired in countless classes, and all the tips we picked up from sewing buddies and friends. It surprises me how many sewing facts, how many "handy hints," a woman can collect in one lifetime.

Until now there haven't been many people to share all this with. Fortunately, for sewists like me, that's changing. A whole new world of garment makers wants to know more, do more, try more, invent more. And when these new sewists feel inspired, they inspire us, too.

I can't tell you how complete I feel when I see a picture on a blog or on Instagram of something some new sewist has made. It makes me infinitely happy to see others enjoy an activity I have loved myself for so long. This also makes me want to start a conversation.

The idea of a conversation is how I have organized this book. A conversation because this book isn't, nor is it intended to be, a complete encyclopedia of sewing or a textbook of any kind. Other folks have written those books and done a very good job.

So there is a bit of a journal in the narrative of this book. I haven't tried to separate how I sew from who I have sewed for or how sewing makes me feel. How could I? Figuring out construction problems and spending an infinite amount of time planning the next project is where my brain has spent most of its time. The techniques included here are among those I have found most useful. If something has helped me, I want to share it with you.

I have also tried to include information that is not regularly repeated elsewhere. I have included random facts I have found pretty interesting, concepts that have helped me work my own way out of a few sewing corners, and a few tactics I made up myself.

So that's how this book works. I have begun with why I think it's a good idea to sew. I have ended with why I think it's an even better idea to keep sewing. In between I have grouped my thoughts into categories I think new and returning sewists think about most. How do you decide what to sew? How do you find a good pattern and what size should it be? How do you make a garment fit? What fabric goes with what pattern? What gear do you really need, and finally, how do you sew so it mostly turns out?

Now you and I both know my answers to these questions are not the last word or even the first one on these subjects. But it's a start and at least mine. Also I have almost come to terms with the reality I can't fit it all into one book. I know I am going to be waking up in the middle of the night a lot in my future with thoughts like "Presser foot … I didn't tell them to raise the presser foot!" or "Seam binding … Why didn't I put in anything about seam binding?"

That's okay. I am reminded that's how sewing works. It's never really finished. Not the fabric and pattern buying, not the scheming and the wardrobe planning and the project contemplating. Not the stitching and the pressing and the failures and the trying-agains. Not the garments that turned out so much better than expected. Not the feeling of power you will have when you know you made it yourself, for yourself, and you did a pretty amazing job of it, too.

Sewing doesn't need to be done, in fact, it's never supposed to be finished. It just feels good to be doing it. In writing this book I have decided what you need from me most is not really the facts or the absolute best of the techniques. Most of that you will figure out on your own. But you need the company of someone who is going that way, too. I am here to get you thinking.

I am here to equip you to be your own problem-solver, because that's what great sewists do, that's what all sewists share.

1 Why Sew?

?

*Every time you fit yourself, you accept yourself—
and it turns out nothing flatters like fit.*

WHEN YOU SEW, I THINK WHAT YOU MAKE MOST OFTEN IS A LIFE, NOT JUST CLOTHES. Sewing is deceptive that way. As an activity, it looks practical and seems sensible. This is just a cover. Sewing gives those who engage in it so much more than something to wear.

Have fun with everyday sewing.

Cotton stretch twill for comfort

Elastic casing that looks like a waistband (page 213)

WHAT SEWING CAN DO FOR YOU

?

Sewing provides a creative outlet for a burning impulse to just make something.

It breaks solitude. It connects us with the souls of generations past, who sewed for themselves and for family, like we do, out of need and with joy. It refills something that ordinary life depletes. And sewing is a pleasure, a real pleasure.

I believe sewing changes you. It adds not just the skill of the craft but skills to your life.

Sewing challenges how the world might make you feel about yourself.

Too tall, too short, too thin, too wide? Sewing lets you take these judgments and minimize them into alterations. Every time you fit yourself, you accept yourself—and it turns out nothing flatters like fit. Sewing puts your presence back under your own control.

Sewing is clear-eyed.

There is something about becoming a maker that makes you look more closely at manufacturing and consumption. Knowing what clothing production entails makes it harder to devalue the time that goes into it or the human price of that labor. Every time any sewist questions the inflated price or the deflated quality of ready-to-wear, she is calling a bluff. Those add up.

Cotton poplin shirt with cut-on sleeves, back yoke, and concealed placket for stripe continuity

Bias-bound sleeve edge instead of hem (page 208)

Sewing retools your brain.

Learning to shift from two to three dimensions is an abstract skill. When you do it, you can feel the shapes move in your head. Flat to round, inside out, right sides together. A sewist can look at the pieces and know how they fit together. That one's a sleeve, darts go in the front, the zipper goes in the back. The curved edge of the collar goes down not up. That long seam means it has to be eased, and that large dot you pivot. Sewing teaches you to think in forms and to read the code without seeing it, sharp in your mind's eye.

Sewing makes you resourceful.

It comes from you, like a web from a spider. If the fabric can be transformed from folded-in-a-bag to a fabulous outfit, it is because you know what to do. You took the time to learn, you practiced, and you figured it out.

Sewing makes you resilient.

Sometimes a project doesn't work out. Sometimes there is a good reason for this and sometimes there is not. But you accept it. You get to understand that mistakes are the practice part of getting better. Best of all, you learn how often the best thing comes after the worst thing and that's why you don't give up.

Sewing gives you a place to put how you feel.

Sew with your heart and your heart is in what you make. Whether it is a button sewn on or a small dress sent in the mail, there is no substitute. Sewists are forever useful.

YOUR PATH TO SEWING

Sewing can give you so much, but learning to sew takes time. It isn't just a matter of finding the right fabric, the right pattern, and following the instructions. You don't just do it; you have to feel it.

You have to feel a <u>need</u> to create strong enough that you will give yourself enough time to find out what kind of sewist you are and what kind of sewing is yours.

We all get there in our own way. My teaching has taught me that there are several different routes into learning to sew. Each new sewist has her (or his) own way in. The right way for each of us is dependent on our own learning styles.

Do You Learn by Reading?

Let's start with the text-based learners. These are the sewists who were often successful and diligent students when they were young. They most certainly had library cards as children and always brought home the notes from school. In a sewing classroom, these same text-based learners are the ones who follow written step-by-step instructions and make their own notes as they go along. Sewists like these pay particular attention to pattern selection. To flourish as sewists, text-based learners will need to work with companies with a reputation for good instructions. They also would do well to invest in some of the classic sewing texts listed in Resources (page 251) for supplementary information.

Do You Learn by Seeing?

Next are the visual learners. These sewists have very active Instagram accounts and skim sewing guide sheets looking for the pictures that tell them what to do. Although they may make more beginner mistakes (because they didn't read the instructions), these sewists are very quick to figure out how to assemble a garment by looking at the pattern piece shapes. These sewists will learn a lot from YouTube tutorials.

Do You Learn by Listening?

Auditory learners are popular participants in any organized sewing class. They interact well and need to hear direction from an instructor, even if that involves a guide sheet being read to them, before they can sew. Auditory learners intuitively gravitate to the social connections of sewing and often make friends with a sewing buddy to sew along with, which works very well. These learners were born to team sew and for sew-alongs.

Do You Learn by Touching?

Tactile sewists seem to most represent sewing as it was traditionally done. These sewists learn literally through touch and are experts at turning a garment inside out to see how it is made. Tactile learners have to handle each piece of fabric in the sewing store. Sewists like these learn best by doing and benefit so much by making samples of new techniques before they tackle an entire garment.

Do It Your Way

I believe what kind of learner you are will determine how you sew. Don't be frustrated if what works for someone else doesn't work for you. Just find a way that does. Accept that there are fast sewists and slow sewists. Understand that there are sewists who measure to the $\frac{1}{16}''$ and those who eyeball instead. Appreciate that there are hand basters and glue stickers; those who use rotary cutters and those who use shears. There is room—a lot of room—to do exactly the kind of sewing you want, using the tools and techniques that feel effective but are comfortable to you.

In sewing, there is not so much a right way, but a way that is right for you.

As you develop your sewing skills, more than anything I want to convey that sewing isn't really difficult at all. I want your sewing to be stress free. I want you to look forward to every project as a process that will stimulate your mind and satisfy your hands.

What to Sew

Forget "saving for good." The good is now.
Give your ordinary life credit ... and clothes.

THERE ARE ONLY TWO RULES: SEW WHAT YOU WILL *REALLY* WEAR, AND SEW IT IN A WAY SO YOU ENJOY THE PROCESS. Your sewing time belongs to you, so protect it.

Simple is chic.

Wrap, snap at one shoulder and out the door

Silk binding instead of facings

Silk charmeuse bow on the shoulder

No zippers or buttons in this dress. Just three armholes!

HOW TO DECIDE

This matters. Too many sewists spend thousands of hours and probably as many dollars on fabric and still say they have "nothing to wear." I know how this feels. Most of us have some sense that what we need is some kind of a wardrobe strategy, not just a clothes-making list. But where do we start? Here are two approaches I find grounding.

The Lifestyle Pie Method

This one is a classic, the first of the reality-check wardrobing strategies. It's a good system for the distracted, so has been helpful to me. The idea is simple. Begin by looking at how you spend your time, paying particular attention to those things you do most often. Walking to work, waiting for kids, knitting and watching Netflix in bed? Come up with a general name for those activities and write them into wedges in a circle, your pie. Finally think about the clothes you need when you do these activities and write that in too, in small letters, within each piece of your pie. Then stand back and have a good look. So this is your real life. Make sure you sew for it.

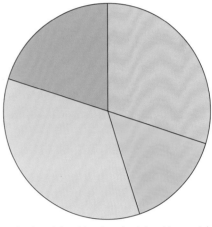

Lifestyle pie example

▪ Sewing: doing, blogging about, teaching, social
▪ Professional: online teaching and radio commentary
▪ Family: childcare, talking, visiting
▪ Exercise: dogwalking, biking, swimming, golfing, social

Of course, this is my own life. It shows large sections for sewing, childcare, and dog walking. My professional-life wedges include teaching online courses and talking on the radio, both activities with a vague dress code. When I saw this, I nixed the new suit. I made a rain hat and a bed jacket instead. You can see how this works.

The Core Wardrobe Method

Like the lifestyle pie method, the idea of a core wardrobe plan is very sensible. It revolves around basics. The idea is to sew enough of the regular units so you always have something decent to wear wherever you go, whatever you do.

So what does this actually look like? The minimalists pare it down. This makes sense. Most minimalists don't seem to me to have closets. The perfect minimalist wardrobe tends to hang as a row on industrial rack in a room with exposed brick—a single pair of jeans, a skirt, pants, a shirt, and a T-shirt. Minimalists also tend stick to the colors gray, black, and white, although they might have a beige trench coat. Seems a bit sparse to me but must making dressing easy. I figure minimalists must do laundry often but I bet they really can pack light when they travel. I am sure they never feel like tourists in New York City.

Another school of core wardrobing begins by wondering, *What would French women wear?* Since most of the folks who worry about this don't seem to be French, I can see why this is a question. The answer is apparently that French women also make use of neutral basics, but expand that a little to include a "little black dress," a cardigan, a camisole, and a lot more accessories—scarves, pearls, and boots in particular. The what-would-French-women-wear style is classic and feminine and makes use of the word iconic a lot. Translating this look to your own life might be a challenge—particularly if your lifestyle pie better illustrates a need to know what-do-women-in-Moose-Jaw-wear.

However, there is common sense to both systems. The strategies of sewing what you really need to wear and of owning a set of backdrop standards are good ones. Even statement lives cannot be entirely reflected by statement pieces, I do know that. But we all have our own context. What we make has to feel creatively interesting and personal. Not every sewist's basics are the same.

So think about how your wardrobe reflects your life for sure, but think too about how it reflects you.

There is something I used to say to career-planning students. Maybe the answer isn't to do what you love, but to do who you are. Clothes might be like that, too.

Consider Personal Style

For many of us, finding our style is a recapturing exercise. With so many voices telling us how to look and what to wear, what's best for us can get lost. But we can get it back. I believe it's there waiting for us in our defaults—the favorite outfits we all put on when we need a lift or some comfort. I think we need to trust the messages of the personal uniform.

WHAT'S YOUR UNIFORM?

You probably have a sense of what this uniform is. The following steps describe what I would do to identify what it might be. This process also will help you put together a real what-to-sew-next list.

1. Go to the closet and find the five to ten things you wear all the time, as in go into the wash and then right back onto your body. Assess what these garments have in common. Comfort (undoubtedly a factor), ease of care (a.k.a. doesn't need ironing), or basics (black pants). Next, assess if these standbys are getting worn. Ask yourself if it's time to replicate these good soldiers with something sharper or fresher or even the same but newer. These are your basics. Sew them first.

2. Make a list of five occasions in the past year when you just wished you had been wearing something else. Ask yourself what would have made you feel more relaxed, confident, or well put together at the time. Base this not on how you wanted to look, but how you wanted to feel at these events. Define those garments. Add them to your priority sewing list.

3. Next, be honest with yourself about what I would call obligation garments. These are the clothes you wear not because you like them, but because you don't have any good reason not to. What do these outfits have in common? Are they just too trendy for you? Uncomfortable? Are they "still good," as my mother would say? Are you keeping them because they represent an investment in fabric and time you don't want to waste? Figure out the common characteristics of these duty garments. Make sure you don't add anything similar to your wardrobe again. Keep your sewing list focused, keep it short, and keep it yours.

WHAT ABOUT FASHION?

A personal style does not negate fashion. Maintaining currency in your clothing says you are current in your head—whenever is *that* not a good thing? But trends need to be handled with discretion.

Keep trying new things, but don't let it override your good sense of what does and doesn't suit your body and your life.

You also need to hit on a trend at the right time to get maximum wear for your efforts. How to do that takes skill. Here I have learned much from my daughter-in-law. Maddie's clothes are classic in color and detail, but she keeps the *outside shape* of her garments on trend. Think about this. Think about updating the *profile* of your uniform basics as a way to keep your style current.

This seems wise. It also helps detect not just what is in style but where styles are going. How do you tell? The hints are in the construction, something sewists already have an eye for. Are sleeves going in or out, dolman or fitted? Where are the shoulder seams shifting? Are pant legs moving straighter, more fitted, or flared? Waists up or down? Are coats loosening up or becoming more fitted? Collars wider or narrower? The early indicators are in the seams; try to see them.

If you can, try not to get too used to the familiar. Keep an open mind. Let your eyes get used to a new look. Once a season, I try to make at least one thing that is different and new to me. I have a hunch that accepting change keeps a person flexible, and I use my clothing to help me I stay that way if I can.

WHOSE CLASSICS?

Sometimes finding your own real style also involves rethinking the classics. I wonder most about blazers, collars on a band, and front-fly trousers—styles borrowed from men. If you are tall and straight-shaped, like I am (or at least used to be), men's styles may suit you. But what if you're not? My observation is that the more curved/female the body shape, the less these "classics" flatter—think of a lapel over a DD bust or a fly zipper over a belly. Why not explore the classics women developed for themselves, such as dresses and Chanel suits? The options are there.

Launching a Sewing Plan

Understanding your style will keep you busy sewing, but it still helps to take aim with a plan. So how does a sewist sew smart? Coordination helps. Some sewists make sure that every new item could be worn with at least one other garment already in their wardrobe. Other sewists are happiest creating outfits one at a time. Both methods work. So also does SWAP ("sewing with a plan"), a system developed by Lynn Cook when she was editor at *Australian Stitches* magazine.

In its purest form, swapping involves sewing 11 pieces that all combine and coordinate:

⊗ 1 jacket / coat / top piece ⊗ 6 tops ⊗ 4 bottoms (skirts or pants)

Color makes this all work. Cook suggests working with two colors for the first basics: the jacket, a top, and two of the bottom garments. She also advises looking for a print in the same two basic colors for a top and bottom to be then worn separately or together so they look like one garment. The remaining bottom garment is made in another coordinating fabric. The remaining four tops can be made in any color you want but, you guessed it, they all must go with all bottoms as well as the jacket.

Now I know this doesn't sound easy to plan and assemble. Many sewists work with more bite-sized versions called mini-SWAPS. For example, I aim for a 4-tops, 2-pants, 1-jacket variation when I travel. However, if you can manage to pull together the whole mix-and-match series of 11 garments (keeping the shapes simple is essential), you can be rewarded with a coherent wardrobe of 48 possibilities. Imagine that. (For more information on what SWAP wardrobes look like, as well as competitive Swapping, see artisanssquare.com.)

The Economics of Sewing

When you sew, there is the likelihood that one day the issue of cost will come up. Maybe someone near and dear might even be old-school enough to ask "are you sure you are saving money with all this sewing?" The real answer to this is "it depends." Decent fabric and patterns don't come cheap. But then again there is no price tag on an enjoyable process, a unique garment, or fit. However, there are some items that are less expensive to make than to buy. In my experience these are:

Vanity clothing   My own rule is the more vulnerable a person feels in the garment, the more they will pay for a good one in ready-to-wear and, consequently, the more money to be saved if you DIY. This category includes lingerie and quality swimwear. Count on being able to make these for at least a third of retail.

Large items that are already expensive   Save money making your own $10 T-shirt? Not so much. An $800 winter coat? Yes. With focus, you can sew a good coat for about $100.

Garments with high-quality details   A sewist can add silk linings, artistic buttons, and bound buttonholes—couture details—at made-at-home costs. Adding these luxuries is one of sewing's greatest pleasures.

AN AUTHENTIC APPROACH TO MAKING CLOTHING

But finally how much can and should you plan what you sew?

I wonder. Sewists are not shoppers, but makers. The clothes we create represent our time and our hopes. Over any sewing plan, I think we need to layer a clear idea of how clothes need to make us feel. What do you want your clothing to say about you? That you are smart and hip? Wise and centered? Ironic and warm? Consider your message. Authentic is its own appropriate.

> **TIP**
>
> **Loving Your Wardrobe**
> The real trick in building a wardrobe you love is not to listen to my mother. Forget "saving for good." The good is now. Give your ordinary life credit ... and clothes.

My Own Oddball Rules for Sewing Contentment

Sometimes I plan; a lot of the time I don't. But I do make decisions, following some personal rules for sewing happiness I have developed over the years.

- If you wouldn't buy it, don't make it.

- Forget sewing like a factory and stash busting. Your fabric collection is an investment. Think like a squirrel in the fall—you never know, you never know.

- Don't cut multiples unless you are really sure—your first priority is to avoid joyless sewing.

⊗ Sew for other people only if you decide you want to make them something; this retains your joy. Hide from folks who say things like, "Would you run up a wedding dress for me?" Just because you can do something doesn't mean you have to.

⊗ If you are frustrated, go to bed. I must do a lot of good sewing in my sleep; it always seems easier in the morning.

⊗ Never spend more time on a project than you will spend wearing it. A dress for the Christmas party is a good example. The vintage pattern three-armhole navy cocktail dress (page 22) is an example—no lining, no zipper, no buttons, and in my simple bound-edge version, no facings. For special occasions, I sew very simply. Exceptions to this rule, of course, are events where there will be pictures taken, such as weddings. In cases like these it might be wise to consider time investment per view in your calculations.

Not everything you make will be a success. I once had a student ask me if I was "trained in Paris." No, I told her, but I do have behind me a mountain of failures that each taught me something. Extract your lesson and move on.

- -

Consider this: You are a creator, not an operator. You are not here to execute anyone else's specs. In the end, the real point is not to build a wardrobe, but to love it.

- -

Barbara's Tips

✓ Coordinating Your Clothing

The easiest way to build a wardrobe that coordinates is to choose a color group and stick to it. Choose either warm or cool colors as a base, and you will be surprised by your many options and how well they go together. Be aware that nearly every color has a warm and a cool version—a tomato red and a blue red, a moss green and a mint green, for example.

✓ Looking Stylish

Think not just about making your clothes but *styling* them. A bracelet-length sleeve really looks best with a bracelet. A pin can draw attention to some great seams. Look to the retro mint dress (page 86), for example. Find the accessories that you feel comfortable in and get them off the dressing table and onto your body. Note though, if you don't like necklaces, you don't have to wear them. I was told by the best obstetrical authority that babies who were delivered by forceps can't stand things around their necks—for life. Maybe that's you.

✓ Choosing Flattering Clothing

- Contrary to old-school wardrobe advice that clothing should be chosen to compensate—for example, that small-busted women should wear ruffled blouses—I maintain that making the most of your assets is the better route. **My own feeling is that a person should dress tighter where she is firmer and looser where she is less firm.** Think this one through.

- Women like me who tend to dress to hide extra weight around the middle have other options that than the usual long loose top. Updated twin sets, a fitted shell with an open cardigan to match, such as the yellow top and cardigan (page 146), meet the same objective but do so while implying a more fitted silhouette.

✓ A Great Trans-Seasonal Garment

One of the handiest trans-seasonal, multipurpose garments anyone can own is a winter white jacket—winter white being any white that has a slight gray cast or is somewhat ivory, as opposed to stark white. Nothing is as useful as an all-around cover-up in the warmer months or is as good at adding snappy style to a dark winter outfit. However, to avoid the lab-coat look, make sure that the fabric has considerable texture—rough silk in a woven or an embossed or ottoman rib knit are my favorites.

✓ Travel

If you travel a lot, nothing beats silk knit. What you spend on fabric you will make back in saved baggage fees. Silk knit drip-dries, it's warm in the winter and cool in the summer, and it's the world's most compressible fabric. Silk wovens can be useful, too. A well-traveled friend always takes a silk sleeping bag liner with her to use when the hotel or hostel sheets look iffy.

✓ Upgrading Your Wardrobe

Never underestimate the power of quality outerwear. **Never underestimate the power of a great coat. It will upgrade everything else you wear.** Over jeans at the grocery store or out in the yard in your pajamas with the dog, a good coat will always make you look polished. My elderly mother once opened her door in the middle of the night to a woman apparently fleeing criminals. When I asked my mother why she took such a risk my mother replied, "She had on a good coat." I rest my case.

3 Finding the Right Pattern

SO MUCH OF SEWING SUCCESS DEPENDS ON THE RIGHT PATTERN. So how does a sewist identify a good pattern? What's the code? What should a sewist look for on the envelope and inside on the guide sheet as indicators to a well-drafted pattern?

Be wary of patterns that are all straight lines, because people aren't.

Fold-over waistline casing

Double-layered self-lined skirt (page 51)

The hem is a fold—no stitches.

CLUES TO A GREAT PATTERN

In the search for the right pattern for a project, it helps to remember that although sewing involves flat fabric and flat paper, a garment is intended for a three-dimensional body. This is key. Be wary of patterns that are all straight lines, because people aren't. Some architectural designs can be beautiful when well drafted, of course, but don't confuse these patterns with ones that are just undeveloped. Sometimes nothing is harder to fit or wear than a "simple-to-sew" pattern.

Also consider pattern pieces and the number of seams.

Get to know your own body's high and low points. Look for seams or darts in these areas so you have a place to fine-tune the fit where you need it.

Don't forget, either, that the greater the adjustment you need to make, the greater the number of seams you will need to distribute the adjustment gradually. For example, you can fit a large bust with less difficulty in a bodice with princess seams than without them. Likewise, a two-piece sleeve is a good solution for a full upper arm. Sewists with a significant difference between waist and hips will find skirts with panels far easier to adjust to flatter than those with just a front and back piece to work with. Remember that sewing a few extra seams is not hard, but trying to recapture fit after a garment is made can be.

Don't place too much store on the fashion drawings or photos on the front of a pattern envelope. Pay more attention to the construction details in the line drawings on the back of the pattern and on the guide sheet. Both are far more informative than the fashion shots on pattern covers.

Self-fabric "ribbing" neck finish

Dolman-sleeve T-shirt

Cover stitched hems.

How to Recognize Pattern Quality

Start by looking at the pattern's line drawings, specifically for features that are indicative of a high-quality pattern. Following are my checklists of important pattern features.

T-SHIRTS OR SIMPLE TOPS

Look for these features:

⊛ Subtle shaping at the side seams. Unless the style lines are meant to be boxy, a great knit T-shirt pattern should have a hint of a waist.

⊛ A sleeve cap shape that is flatter and longer at the back and has slightly more curve at the front. Feel your own shoulder and you will understand why this is important.

⊛ A front neckline lower than the back neckline. Necks bend forward, so this one is just makes sense.

⊛ An opportunity for bust shaping. The larger the bust, the more important this is. Patterns with different cup-size options, or princess seams, are excellent. Any *woven* "T-shirt" pattern should have bust darts for a smooth fit, in my opinion. Also, a *fitted* knit T-shirt generally needs a little extra length in the front. During construction, this length will be eased in at the side seams for bust ease.

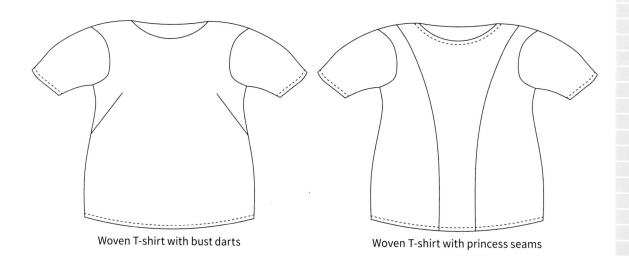

Woven T-shirt with bust darts   Woven T-shirt with princess seams

SHIRTS, BLOUSES, AND OTHER STRUCTURED TOPS

Look for these pattern features:

⊗ Seams along areas that might need adjusting. Specifically, I look for front darts or princess seams. Many shirt patterns have both—darts in the front and princess seams in the back, or sometimes French darts both front and back. Very useful.

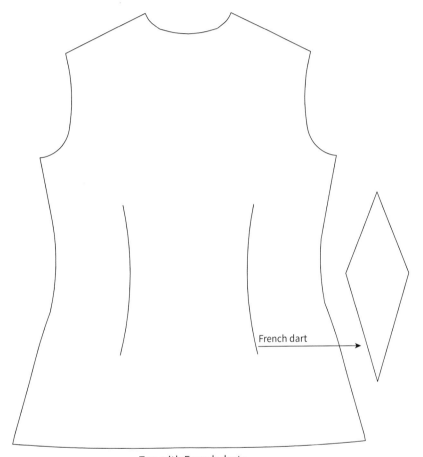

French dart

Top with French darts

⊗ Shirt collars with a separate stand and collar. The cut-all-in-one units ignore the fact that the grain of a stand and a collar need to be slightly different to do their jobs—one to hold up and one to roll. The seam between a collar and stand also makes a break line that helps a collar fold down nicely. In addition, the collar stand pattern piece should be curved and the collar edge should have a curve, too, as necks have a slope.

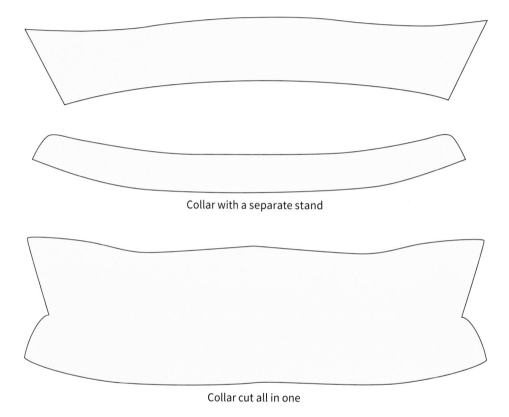

Collar with a separate stand

Collar cut all in one

⊗ A proper shirt placket above the cuffs in shirt sleeves (reference a man's shirt), not a continuous lap. Real plackets lie much flatter.

DRESSES

Look for these pattern features:

⊗ Seams and/or darts anywhere where fit might need to be adjusted.

⊗ A center back seam in the absence of back darts, even in a sheath dress. Human backs have a natural curve, and omitting an opportunity for even slight shaping is a guarantee of a baggy back dress.

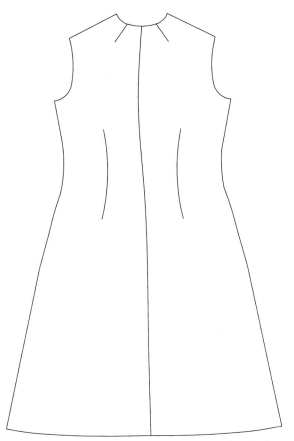

Dress, center back seam, French darts, and back neck darts

⊗ Back neck darts to accommodate a forward neck. As long as the population is going to spend more time looking down at computers than marching in parades, we are going to need these.

JACKETS AND COATS

Look for these pattern features:

⊗ Separate upper and lower collar pieces. Having both creates a nicer collar roll in heavier fabrics. A two-piece under-collar is ideal, too. This means the under-collar can be cut on the bias from center out, in two pieces, for a more flexible roll.

⊗ A two-piece sleeve with an extra vertical seam to allow for easing and shaping at the elbow. This is really important. Look at your own arm. Even relaxed there is a slight bend at the elbow. A good-looking sleeve should do the same.

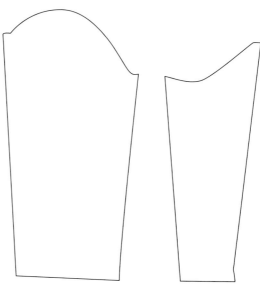

Two-piece sleeve. The extra vertical seam allows for easing and shaping at the elbow.

⊗ Separate lining pieces. Don't compromise on this. A duplicate of main pattern pieces doesn't do the job. A lining is cut differently than the garment body for ease over construction details, with raised armholes and lifted shoulder lines, for example. Wearing ease in a lining also is created by a pleat at the center back for movement and extra for folds along the hemlines so the hems won't pull up. You can draft your own lining pattern of course—the odd trend towards impractical unlined coat patterns requires it—but to me this seems a nuisance and an imposition on the pattern purchaser.

⊗ Front facings. Open jackets without closures have encouraged patterns with lining to the edge, but don't fall for it. Without structure, any front edge wants to flip to the right side. An interfaced facing stops this. An exception to this advice is of course a Chanel jacket, which is well structured with handwork and another story all together.

SKIRTS

Look for these pattern features:

⊗ Waistbands with a curve. Also look for a similar shape in the waistline of the skirt. Beware of rectangle waistbands—they will just crease or stand up at the sides. The same advice holds true for waistbands on pants patterns.

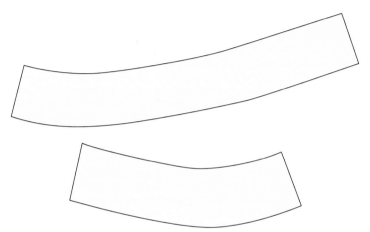

Note the difference between a conventional straight waistband and a two-piece curved waistband

⊗ Back darts longer than the front darts. For the best fit over real curves, four darts rather than two darts front and back also make for the smoothest fit.

⊗ Center back and center front seams in A-line skirt patterns. These seams are needed to allow the weight-bearing grain to be maintained over the legs and centered on the body. Without these seams, such as in a flared skirt with the front laid on the fold, the grain will just hold out the sides of the skirt stiffly in points.

NOW WHAT ABOUT PANTS PATTERNS?

Unfortunately, there isn't a simple checklist for finding the right pants pattern. Most sewists will tell you that finding a pants pattern that fits can be a real challenge. Unlike other garments, where the issues are limited to horizontal and vertical fit, pants intersect the body. So much comes down to crotch curve draft.

The great news, however, is that *so* many pants-fitting issues can be solved or close to solved once the sewist has found a pattern company that drafts to a shape like hers. There are real differences.

As a general rule, many of the big North American companies draft a front and back crotch shape similar in angle and not majorly different in length. This draft suits many women, particularly those who do not have very significant differences between their own front and back contours and lengths. On the other hand, some of the independent and European pattern companies tend to draft very different front and back crotches—with the back crotches longer and more acutely angled and front crotches noticeably shorter and flatter. This draft works better for women who have a very defined rear shape and very significant differences between front and back crotch lengths. In the illustration below, you can see the difference between an independent crotch draft on the left and a Big Four pattern company draft on the right.

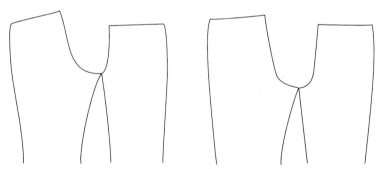

The crotch shape on the left would fit a body with a round rear;
the shape on the right would fit a more balanced body type.

So to find a good pants pattern, you are going to have to experiment with pattern companies to find one that seems to have a block closest to your shape. This will take some time, patience, and optimism, but is worth doing. I now have two go-to pattern companies for pants that seem to draft to my crotch curve. For more on how to assess your own crotch profile and how to find a close match in a purchased pattern, see Chapter 4: If It Fits, They Will Wear It (page 60).

HOW TO START IF YOU'RE A BEGINNER

What Is an Easy Pattern?

New or returning sewists sometimes say this to me: "Is this pattern too hard?" or "I am learning so I just need something easy. What do you suggest?"

I always hesitate before I answer questions like these. I don't like to underestimate anyone.

New sewist after new sewist has taught me that the desire to learn and keep moving past the frustrations can be a stronger indicator of a great result than years of experience.

However, there *are* some patterns that are easier than others for sewing newbies. First don't believe any pattern-maker's statement that any pattern is "perfect for beginners" or an "easy sew." Some of the trickiest patterns I have ever made were labeled that way. What these descriptions usually really mean is that the pattern has a limited number of pattern pieces. Having fewer pieces is not a guarantee of simplicity of construction and certainly not fit. That said, I do think there are some categories of patterns that are easier for sewists who are learning.

Hallmarks of a Good Pattern for Beginners

Clean lines   This doesn't mean fewer pattern pieces, but it does mean the seams don't have many angles or strong curves. Gathering, easing in (as in princess seams and tailored sleeves), pivoting, and inserts (as in a front yoke) take practice and can be overwhelming for someone making their first garment.

If you are learning, try to limit the number of new techniques per garment. To begin with, aim for body-skimming or fairly loose fit as opposed to a body-conscious style. Fitting is a whole skill set on its own and best mastered once you are comfortable with basic sewing techniques. Take it one step at a time. Let yourself feel good about each step before moving on.

It can be made in a plain weave natural fiber   Cotton, wool, and linen are great fabrics for beginners. They press well and the layers tend to hold still together once pinned.

I would definitely hold off on anything slippery for quite a while.

About starting with knits, I am of two minds. Tactile learners—potters rather than illustrators—might do fine starting with a T-shirt because these fabrics are sewn more by feel than by measurement. Other sewists—text-based and visual learners, for example—might find the predictability of wovens more reassuring starting out.

For more on fabric choice, see Chapter 6: Choosing and Cutting Fabric (page 116).

Great instructions   Experienced sewists have a repertoire of techniques in their heads to draw on, but new sewists need things spelled out. The best instructions teach as well as direct. Look for instructions that are well illustrated and tell you *why* you do things, not just what to do.

You can detect this in a guide sheet that is broken down with headings, not a long list of discouraging directives, such as "Step 178: Now turn the sleeve to the right side...."

Check out well-established independent pattern lines—such as Cutting Line Designs (cuttinglinedesigns.com) and Jalie (jalie.com)—for good instructions. Some of the sewing pattern magazines, such as *Ottobre Design* (ottobredesign.com/en/), have interesting techniques, too.

Progress through Patterns as You Learn—A Learning Plan

Learning to sew is done one garment at a time. So if the learning is to be progressive, each new garment should introduce a new technique.

If I were to design a learning path for new sewists, this is what it would look like:

1. A skirt. The fitting of a skirt is minimal and is focused on the waistline and side seams. To begin, try an elastic-waist skirt just to get used to laying out a pattern on grain, using the machine, and seam finishing.

Next, try a simple A-line skirt for practice sewing and pressing darts, interfacing a waistband, and installing an invisible zipper. For why I think invisible zippers are the easiest zippers to put in, see Chapter 7: The Gear Side of Sewing (page 144).

2. A shift-type dress with sleeves in a firm knit, such as a double-knit fabric (a double-knit called *ponte* may work well) sewn on a regular machine. Since most of us wear a lot of knits, I wouldn't hold off on these too long. After the detail of a skirt, a dress like this will feel easy, which makes you feel smart … and that's good.

This dress will help you get comfortable with sleeve shapes and adjusting stitch width at the sewing machine. You should use a very narrow zigzag for seams, and you might also try a twin-needle hem (page 159).

Next, you could try a T-shirt in a more stretchy knit fabric. Both these garments are very wearable.

3. A blouse or top with buttons, short or three-quarter sleeves, and a convertible collar, as opposed to a shirt-style collar with a band. Learning to stitch and press a collar, sew a front facing, set in sleeves, and make buttonholes will put you into the big leagues. Do this and you will feel like you can pretty much do anything. You might even try a patch pocket here, too.

From these three garment types, you can move on to shirts or blouses with cuffs, dresses with waists, more darts and facings, jackets (linings are easy), and then pants.

I suggest pants last because some sewists get stalled in fitting issues and it might be necessary to experiment a little to find a pattern that suits you. Pull-on stretch woven or knit pants are easiest for starters. Pants with fly fronts and jeans are more time-consuming and complex.

WHEN TO IGNORE THE PATTERN DIRECTIONS

Whatever your level of skill, you can make a great pattern even better if you have the confidence to think for yourself when you read pattern instructions.

Just like you can perfect a pattern by fine-tuning the fit, you can also refine pattern instructions to streamline the construction process and improve results. Use your critical thinking skills. Learn from the ready-to-wear in your closet. Be comfortable making your own technical updates.

MINI LESSON

Eliminating a Bulky Front Shirt Band

Look for opportunities to eliminate bulk every time two straight pieces are sewn together. As an example, compare your woman's shirt pattern with a man's ready-to-wear shirt. Note the differences in the front bands. Chances are your woman's pattern has separate, interfaced, sewn-on button and buttonhole bands. These can be very bulky and stiff. By contrast, a man's shirt has simple bands created by two simple folding techniques: one side folded under twice for buttons, the other folded to the right side twice for button-holes. This is a technique worth borrowing.

To replicate this yourself in a shirt, use a fabric that doesn't have a definite right and wrong side. Just add a cut-on exten-sion twice the width of a finished band to each front. On the button side of the shirt, fold this extension to the wrong side twice and stitch close to the folded edge.

On the buttonhole side, fold the exten-sion twice to the right side of the shirt and topstitch along both long edges.

Since the fabric is folded double on both sides, you do not need extra interfacing. The finished look is more professional than a sewn-on band and looks far less rigid on the body or over a bust.

PATTERN CHANGES FOR SEWING KNITS

It also makes sense to cast a critical eye over any instructions for sewing knits. For some strange reason, instructions for these fabrics are often written as if they were intended for woven, not knit, fabrics and will produce disappointing results.

In particular, watch for and *don't* follow instructions that tell you ...

... to sew a knit seam with two rows of straight stitches for strength.
Instead, use a serger if you have one, or use a simple line of small zigzags—a perfect seam for knits. I use a zigzag stitch 0.8 wide and 2.5 long.

... to press and sew, press and sew.
Too much pressing just stretches these fabrics permanently out of shape. When pressing knit fabric, think how you would handle a hand knit. Press only lightly and minimally, generally at the end of the project.

... to finish seam allowances.
Knits don't fray; this is unnecessary.

... to straight stitch around a neckline band to finish.
This can so easily break when stretched. You don't need it.

CONSIDER GOING PATTERNLESS

Sometimes not using a pattern at all is a real option, at least for a detail if not for a whole garment.

I do this a lot. Look for areas in a garment that seem to have multiple pattern pieces (the front band example on page 49 was one) and see if you can substitute a fold for a seam. Fewer layers, producing a smoother exterior, is so important to a professional-looking garment.

PATTERNLESS IDEA
Hemless Knit Skirt

One of my favorite patternless projects is a hemless, knit straight skirt. This technique is perfect for straight skirts in a fabric that may be too light to support a nice hem or may need to be lined. This is such an easy way to sew a fast, casual, knit skirt.

1. Measure your desired finished skirt hip measurement. In a knit, this can be the same as your actual hip or 2″–3″ larger. For a very fitted skirt, remember knits stretch, so the skirt can even be cut with negative ease, meaning even an inch or so narrower than your body measurement. Divide the skirt measurement number you settle on by 2 because you will need a skirt front and a skirt back. Add the equivalent of 2 seam allowances. Cut your skirt pieces to this width measurement.

2. Decide how long you want your finished skirt to be. Multiply this times 2 (since the hem of this skirt is on the fold, you need skirt pieces twice as long as the finished skirt) and add twice the width needed for an elastic casing. For example, to easily accommodate 1″ elastic, add 1½″ casings to each skirt piece or 3″ to the total length of the piece.

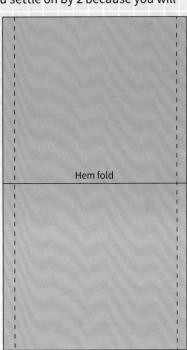

Hem fold

Both your skirt pieces need to be cut to this length measurement.

3. Construct the skirt by sewing the front to back at the side seams, creating a long tube.

4. "Hem" the skirt by folding this tube up on itself, wrong sides together. Baste the 2 raw edges at the top together. Here is what that fold that has become the hem looks like:

5. Finish by turning the top of the skirt under, in the case of a 1″ elastic under 1½″, and topstitching down, using a zigzag stitch, a multistep zigzag, a twin needle, or a coverhem. Leave a gap in the stitching to insert the elastic. Join the elastic ends and close the gap in the stitching to complete.

Done. No hem to do because the fold has become the hem and, of course, the skirt is now fully lined, too.

PATTERNLESS IDEA

Vintage-Style Pleat

I picked up this idea from my vintage pattern collection, and it can be used to add a box pleat to the center front of any A-line skirt pattern or a kick pleat to the back of any straight-skirt pattern. With this technique, a closed pleat at the back of a skirt will nicely cover all lining details and a slip, if you are one of the few women left who still, like me, wear one.

The concept is simple. Rather than sewing the kick pleat using the extra pleat pattern pieces, simply lay the back skirt pattern piece next to the folded length of fabric, arranging the pattern so the center back seam is a half-pleat distance away from the fold line. This allows you to cut the pleat and skirt all in one seamless piece.

Here's how to make a cut-on kick pleat:

1. Decide how wide you want the finished pleat to be. For a finished pleat about 6″ long and 3½″ wide, move the pattern piece back 1¾″ (3½″ divided by 2) from the fold of fabric.

2. Cut out the back pattern piece. In this example, cut down along the center back cutting line; but when you are 6″ from the hem fold, cut out horizontally to the fold. This box cut on the fold of fabric will become the pleat.

3. To construct the pleat, stitch the skirt's center back seam, but switch to a long basting stitch when you are about ⅝″ below the cut edge where the pleat box starts. Continue machine basting to the bottom of the skirt.

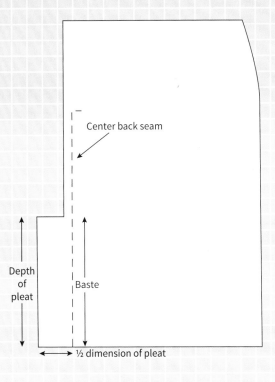

Center back seam

Depth of pleat

Baste

½ dimension of pleat

4. Next, working from the right side, spread and flatten the pleat evenly on either side of the basted seam. Press. From the right side, topstitch to close the top of the pleat to hold it in place, drawing in stitching lines first with chalk for accuracy if you want.

5. Hem the skirt and then—this is a great trick to make sure pleats hold their shape—edgestitch the inner folds of the pleat right up through the hem and as far as you can sew.

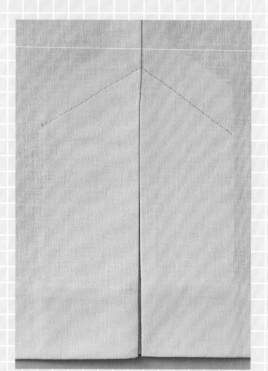

A box pleat in the front of a skirt is made exactly the same way.

PATTERNLESS IDEA

Lined Patch Pocket

Opportunities for patternless sewing also can be found in places where one piece needs to fit another. In lining a patch pocket, I often do not cut out the lining as per the pattern piece. Instead, I use this lining technique when I have to sew a patch pocket with a rounded bottom. Stitching around a curved edge is so much less stressful than burning your fingers trying to evenly press under seam allowances.

1. Pin a hunk of lining fabric right sides together at the top of the pocket piece. Stitch the lining to the pocket piece, making a break in this stitching so you have an opening to use later to turn the pocket.

2. Press the seam down toward the lining. Press the hem allowance down along the fold line.

3. Turn the piece over. Following the shape of the pocket piece, stitch completely around the pocket.

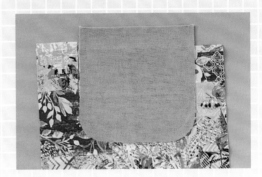

4. Cut the lining piece to match the pocket shape. Note the dots indicating the opening left in the stitching for turning the pocket.

5. Turn the pocket through the gap in the hem stitching, and press the pocket. The opening can be closed later by hand or caught in topstitching the hem from the right side.

PATTERNLESS IDEA

Easy Zippered Pocket

Be alert for many tiny pattern pieces that must be precisely fitted together, often with small seam allowances. A classic case is in the insertion of a zippered pocket, a detail so often added to an otherwise simple bag pattern or jacket. Rather than being concerned about all that marking, about zipper facings, and about making sure both pocket bag pieces line up, I use my own dependable "hunk of fabric" method, always with great results.

1. Pin a large hunk of lining fabric right sides together over the garment, centered on the pocket area, matching grainlines, and with the zipper area in the middle of this fabric. Mark the stitching box for the zipper but no other marking on the hunk of fabric. You can use an ordinary pencil or fabric marker to do this. What I do most often is pin a piece of small-square graph paper (as in 8-squares-to-the-inch graph paper) to the fabric and follow the lines.

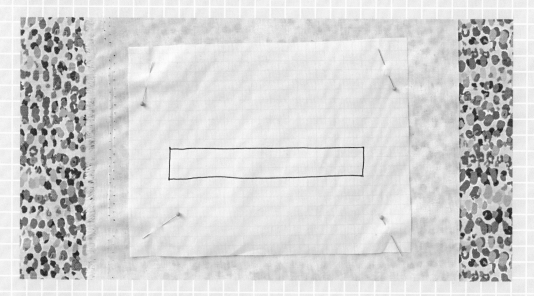

2. Stitch around the box, using short stitches (1.5 or so) and starting the stitching somewhere in the middle of a long side so the corners are not weakened. If you are using graph paper as a marking guide, the short stitches will also make it very easy to tear the paper away once the stitching is done

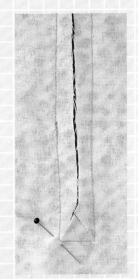

3. Cut along the centerline through all layers, stopping before the end and cut to the corners creating 2 large triangles at each end. Make the triangles biggish so you have something to hold onto. If the thought of cutting through those layers scares you, just put a pin diagonally across the corner as a safety bar.

4. Turn the lining through the opening and press the box so it is a neat rectangular opening. Clip into the corners again if you see any puckering there. Hand baste the edges to hold them still and to roll the lining fabric to the inside and press.

5. Place the zipper behind this opening and topstitch around all edges of the box to secure it. Note that you can hand baste the zipper into position or use sewist's basting tape.

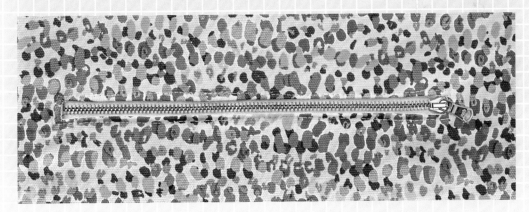

6. Now working from the wrong side, just let the top layer of the hunk of fabric fall down naturally, pin the edges together, mark a pocket shape, and stitch the pocket bag through both layers, folding the garment fabric out of the way as you stitch to make this easier. Trim away any excess and finish the raw edges.

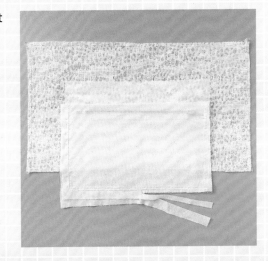

Now how neat is that?

Barbara's Tips

✓  **Interpreting Pattern Marks**

Pattern notches have meaning and this is useful knowledge when assembling many pieces. Single notches are placed on front seamlines, double notches on side seams, and triple notches on center back seams.

✓  **Using Your Tape Measure**

Old-school measuring tapes are often ⅝″ wide and can be used to quickly add seam allowances to new pattern pieces or traced patterns.

Starting Your Own Collections

- TNT is short for "tried 'n' true" pattern, generally a basic garment that is perfected in fit and with logical construction steps. For those with design aspirations, TNTs are a great place to start. The garments in this book were made from a limited repertoire of favorite patterns, my TNTs.

- If you find a detail you like, start a collection. I have a large envelope called "pockets" and another called "collars" where I keep my favorite used pattern pieces and can add to new patterns.

Sewing Children's Clothing

When sewing for babies, children, or those with mobility challenges, always opt for raglan, rather than set-in sleeve styles. A raglan armhole is much larger and this makes maneuvering while dressing much easier.

4

If It Fits, They Will Wear It

As any woman who was ever in junior high knows, there is little relationship between a girl's build and the size of her breasts. In fit, it is build that matters.

YEARS AGO, WHEN I WHEN WORKED AT AN AUSTRALIAN TECH COLLEGE, I DECIDED TO OFFER AN EXTRACURRICULAR COURSE ON BASIC SEWING. Two of my students were twin brothers, welders in fact, who described sewing as "exactly like sheet-metal work, mate. You cut her out flat and you make her round." Exactly. That process of flat to round is what sewing to fit is all about.

Every sewist needs a sewing outfit!

Stretch bengaline slim pants

A TNT pattern also used for the turquoise pants (page 14)

THE TRUTH ABOUT MOST PATTERN SIZING

Before you start unfolding those tightly packed sheets of pattern tissue paper, let's talk about fit as an idea. To do that we will need to take some basic body measurements and assess what kind of "round" you are.

Making clothes that look and feel comfortable isn't really all that hard. But the truth is that no pattern can fit every body shape right out of the envelope.

However, it is possible to zero in on the best size match. First, let's pull back the curtain on a few pattern realities.

Significant Fact 1: Pattern Companies Haven't Always Been Realistic

On the back of every commercial sewing pattern, or on the envelope flap, is a tiny print little chart of body measurements and sizes. Most sewists search these charts for the right size or multisize pattern to buy. This is the point at which things start to fall apart.

Listen, nobody has those same measurements, not lined up in a row in a single size. It's not you, it's them. I was once told that standard sizing had been based on the strange assumption that the average woman has a hip measurement half her height. True or not, this story does have some credence when you look at most pattern company measurement charts. Take size 8, not an uncommon size. In major-brand pattern land, size 8 has a waist size of 24″ and a hip of 33½″. Now tell me, who do you know past the age of eight that has 33½″ hips? Measurements like that are from the era when women died in childbirth.

Cotton print top with stand collar

Let's move up. Apparently, the average North American woman is a size 16. Okay, now sewing patterns are often considered by a lot of woman to run larger than ready-to-wear. So let's look at the body measurements for size 16—bust of 38″, hip of 40″ (which is a maybe at best), and a waist of 30″. Thirty inches—that's 1″ more than 29″. Not exactly your standard North American woman's waist.

We are back to it's not you, it's them. What then are you to do?

Let's start with what *not* to do. First, don't try to average it out and work from a pattern size that seems to fall in between your largest and smallest measurement. This is your best guarantee that you will get a garment that won't fit well anywhere at all.

The better approach, and the one you should use if you are going to develop into an excellent pattern fitter, is to buy a pattern that has only one of your actual body measurements printed on it, and learn how to adjust the rest.

The trick, of course, is what measurement should you choose as your priority measurement? This brings us to Significant Fact 2.

Significant Fact 2: It Is Always, Always Easier to Make a Pattern Larger Than It Is to Make It Smaller

"Just take it in" might seem like prudent advice, but it ignores the fact that there is a lot more going on in a garment than side seams. Armholes and necklines, for example, are cut out larger in a larger size, and once something is cut out, it's gone. Reducing a neck opening at this point would be impossible.

To really zero in on an appropriate size, think frame. Your central core—made of spine, shoulders, and pelvic structure—is your unique constant. That's what you have to match as closely as possible to find the right size for you.

From that point, anything else you need to add, you can add around this core. So select a pattern for your bones, not your weight. Easy.

Think of where your frame most contacts a garment, too. In most cases, you are going to be selecting a pattern that either hangs from or is supported by the upper body (blouse, top, coat, jacket, or dress) or the lower body (pants, shorts, or skirts). It is so important to focus on a measurement/pattern match for the part of the body that is going to support the garment. For example, if the garment is going to fall from your shoulders, select a pattern closest to your smallest upper body measurement, almost always your upper chest rather than your bust or waist. If the garment is going to fall from your lower body, select a pattern by the closest match to your smallest lower body measurement. Depending on your body type, this may be either your hips or your waist.

In any and either case, by choosing your patterns this way, you are sticking to the it's-easier-to-make-a-pattern-larger-than-smaller rule, and you have already eliminated many of your fitting issues.

WHAT TO MEASURE, HOW TO DO IT, AND WHY

There are many good resources on how to take detailed body measurements. I have provided a Personal Measurement Chart (pages 76 and 77) that you can copy and fill out. But before you run for the measuring tape, let's talk about a few key measurements and why I think they are very important.

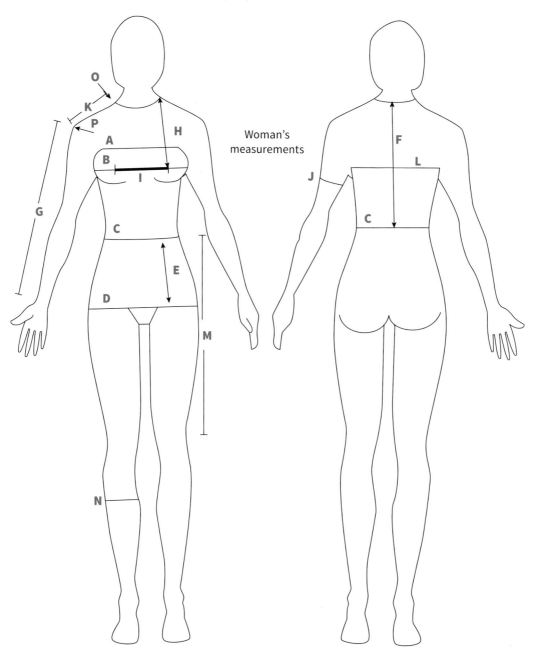

Woman's measurements

A. Upper chest/bust

B. Full bust

C. Operational waist

D. Widest lower body measurement

E. Distance from waist to widest measurement

F. Back waist length

G. Arm length

H. Bust depth

I. Bust span

J. Bicep width

K. Shoulder length

L. Back width

M. Waist to knee

N. Calf width

O. Neck point

P. Shoulder point

Basic Measurements

UPPER CHEST / UPPER BUST VERSUS BUST

I have an interesting fact for you. Men's and children's patterns always refer to chest measurements, but women's patterns list bust. I am not sure why this is the case; perhaps someone in pattern land got coy, but what you really need to measure first is your upper body frame, *not* your bust. As any woman who was ever in junior high knows, there is little relationship between a girl's build and the size of her breasts. In fit, it is build that matters.

You will find this accurate upper body/frame measurement by wrapping a measuring tape up high above your breasts, just under your armpits. The measuring tape likely will not be parallel to the floor. In fact, if it crosses nicely over your shoulder blades, it will move up from under your armpits a bit over your chest. Don't stress too much; you are just trying to make a dress, not build a rocket. This measurement will catch your bones and capture the muscles and whatever else you have going on independent of your breast size.

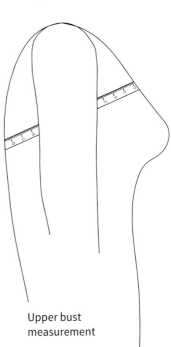

Upper bust measurement

Use *this* measurement, which is most usually much smaller than your "full bust," as the one to use when choosing your pattern. Just substitute the measurement for upper bust as bust in your head when you look at the size chart on the pattern envelope.

Making a good match here for the "hanger" for any upper body garment minimizes the overall alteration work you need to do from here on, often minimizing it to just adding on what you need elsewhere further down the line—easy stuff.

WAIST—OPERATIONAL VERSUS ANATOMICAL WAISTLINE

Waistlines are the mirage elements of fit—more of a concept than a place. Where to measure for a waistline is a tough one, and in my experience there is no other place on the human body where people are so particular about what feels right to them.

My best advice is to make a decision about where you feel your waistline is and to make this your operational waist, the measurement you can transfer or check against your pattern.

The Widest Lower Body Measurement (a.k.a. Often but Not Always Your Hips)

To make clothes you can move in, it is necessary to find your maximum lower body width. Where this is varies. Some of us have good childbearing hips and some of us just have good obstetricians. Some of us are curvier in the side view and flattest straight on. Some of us get widest just below our navels, and others carry things lower, cowgirl-style, in saddlebags. It doesn't matter.

What matters is that you find your own widest point and measure it. Forget about looking for a "hip measurement." Just wrap a measuring tape around your waist and let it out as you slide it down your body. When you find you need to tighten up the tape again, you know you have just passed your widest spot.

HIP / WIDEST PART DISTANCE FROM THE WAIST

Mark where you find your widest part for future reference; you might try a permanent marker or a tattoo. Measure how far away it is from your waistline. If you add to lower body width, it is very important that you make these additions exactly at the point where you will need them most.

BACK WAIST LENGTH

Unlike width measurements, which are incorporated into patterns plus design and wearing ease, all body length measurements can be compared literally to pattern pieces. This is handy. Take your back waist measurement by bending your head forward slightly so you can feel the prominent bone at the back of your neck. Measure from this bone down your spine to your waist. Compare this measurement to the pattern or to the back waist length listed on the pattern envelope as a basis for any necessary bodice length additions or subtractions.

Less Usual but Crucial Measurements and Information

ARM LENGTH

Men's shirt makers have given this clear attention and sell shirts by sleeve length as well as collar size. Designers of women's clothes and patterns seem to have passed this one by. To find your arm length, measure from the bone you can feel at the end of your shoulder (the place where a shoulder seam sits) to just covering your wrist bone. When you take this measurement, make sure your arm is relaxed with the elbow naturally bent, the way it will be in a sleeve, and not held stiff and straight down your side.

BUST DEPTH

Darts and shaped seamlines, such as princess seams, are geared to take fabric in where you don't need it and let it out again where you do. Situating this right makes the difference between an outfit that makes you feel snappy and one with pouchy things in some places and tight little wrinkles in others. Knowing your neck point to bust high point measurement is crucial.

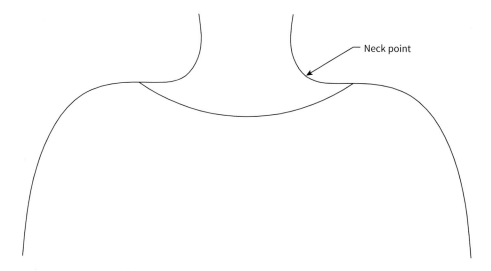

Neck point

1. Identify the spot where your shoulder seam meets your neckline. If you have drawn your shoulder seam onto your body with permanent marker, as I might suggest, this will be easy. This is the midline on the top of your shoulder.

2. Locate your "jewel neckline," which is the standard circle neckline that you could reasonably and comfortably wear. This is where the jewel part comes in. Find a simple necklace (or make one yourself out of small paper clips—children are helpful here) and put it around your neck. The exact place where your shoulder seam meets your necklace is your neck point.

3. Measure directly down in a straight line from your neck point, where your necklace and shoulder seam intersect, to your nipple. Write it down. You now have the all-important "bust depth" measurement. This will save your darts.

BUST SPAN

Measure right across from nipple to nipple. Write it down. As princess seams are designed to run right over your high-point-we-really-mean-nipple, this is very useful information to have when altering patterns to fit.

UPPER ARM / BICEP WIDTH

I like to take this measurement with the arm flexed, Popeye-style.

Since the usual ease allowed in a sleeve is 1½″–2″, a quick comparison between this measurement and the pattern will tell you if any sleeve-width additions or subtractions are needed.

SHOULDER LENGTH

I find this measurement interesting as it can vary so much between women of a similar build, between 4½″–5¾″ in my experience. Take this measurement from the edge of your "jewel neckline" to the end of the triangular bone you can feel at the end of your shoulder when you raise your arm slightly.

You should adjust your shoulder length at the end of the shoulder where it meets the sleeve seam. Getting shoulder length right is critical to a sleeve that fits and hangs well.

BACK WIDTH

If you are wearing a standard–size garment, you will know if adjustments to back width are necessary when you reach forward with your arms.

This measurement is taken straight across and flat right across the upper back, from arm crease to arm crease, taking care not to measure under the arm in any way. In addition to a naturally broad back, this measurement also catches the rounded back that so many of us have acquired at our desks.

WAIST TO KNEE

Obviously, this measurement is useful when checking skirt lengths. It is also helpful when sewing pants. Almost all pant profiles, straight from the hip excepted, start tapering or flaring at knee level. Lengthening or shortening the leg length by adjusting at the knee, rather than at the hem, will allow you to make length adjustments without losing the style of the pant.

CALF WIDTH

If you are a person who buys wide-calf boots, like me, skinny jeans have been a reminder that this is a measurement worth taking. Measure your calf at the widest part. Make sure the below-the-knee width of any narrow pants you make in stretch wovens is no less than this measurement, or at least 2″ wider when working with nonstretch fabrics. Note that leggings and other two-way knit pants can be the same as or even less than your calf measurement.

And Now to Paraphrase Einstein: Not Everything That Counts Can Be Counted

In addition to the quantifiable realities of your figure, you need to assess the general landscape of your body to achieve an ace fit. Here are some body areas worth pondering.

SHOULDER SLOPE

After many years of watching sewing students fret because their blouses didn't fit, I finally figured out how important individual shoulder shape was. What makes shoulder slope interesting is that these fitting issues don't seem to focus on the shoulders at all but are transferred to general comfort around necklines and sleeves.

A sewist with square shoulders might not see her own shoulders as the cause, but she knows her collars ride up and she sees pull lines across the collarbone. Another sewist with what one student called her sloping "duck shoulders" will have the opposite problem with necklines—they will slide down the arm and vertical folds will hang in the upper bodice. Do a quick bathroom mirror visual check and decide if you have regular, square, or sloping shoulders.

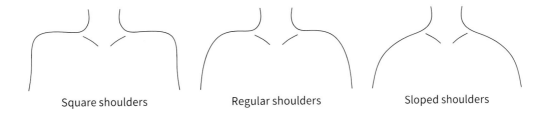

Square shoulders   Regular shoulders   Sloped shoulders

NECK ANGLE

Computers, short children, and time spent sacrificing posture to life has given many of us necks that curve forward. If you can identify this in yourself, look for patterns with back neck darts already built in, or learn to add them to patterns that don't.

SOFT TISSUE DISTRIBUTION

The importance of that which is neither bone nor muscle needs no introduction. Measuring tape numbers assume we are all evenly distributed around our bodies. Of course, this just isn't true. A woman with a broad back and an average cup size, for example, may have the same "bust" measurement as her smaller sister with a bigger bust and a smaller frame. It makes no sense to expect the same pattern size to fit them both.

So before you start adding inches to any pattern piece, consider where those inches really need to be added. Have a good look at your side and back view as well as your front. Take pictures if you want to face the truth. The object of this exercise is to make sure your garments place fabric where you need it to be. This is the time to consider how that fabric can be shaped to fit your own body. Pay particular attention to the aim and placement of potential darts, and take measurements that will help you position them. Think about where a dart needs to aim—anywhere from ¾"–1" away from the Three B's (bust, belly, and butt)—and how long a dart needs to be to do that. Also consider places where you might not need the darts a pattern suggests, between a waistline and a full belly, for example, and make a note to eliminate those.

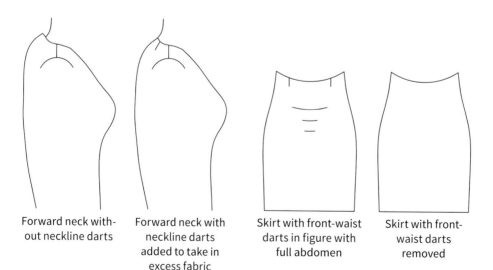

| Forward neck without neckline darts | Forward neck with neckline darts added to take in excess fabric | Skirt with front-waist darts in figure with full abdomen | Skirt with front-waist darts removed |

Wearing Ease

Wearing ease is the extra space you need to have between the garment's measurements and your actual body measurement, so you can ... say ... sit down without splitting your pants.

How much wearing ease is a personal choice, but generally 2″ at the bust, 1+″ at the waist, and 2″–3″ at the hips. Note that more wearing ease is necessary for larger figures, less for smaller and tauter figures.

To estimate a comfortable wearing ease for a skirt, put a tape measure around your hips and sit down. The difference between your sitting and standing measurements would be your own wearing ease. For firm figures this may be 2″, for fuller figures 4″. When you make any pattern adjustments, always make sure you have allowed yourself the appropriate wearing ease.

Design is extra fabric a designer may add, on top of wearing ease, to express a design—for example, adding inches for pleats or many inches for a swing coat. Negative ease refers to a garment cut smaller than your body measurements in knit fabrics. Negative ease is used in activewear, swimwear, lingerie, T-shirts, or other garments where a close fit is desirable.

PERSONAL MEASUREMENT CHART

Tracking your vertical and horizontal measurements and body shape considerations is a start. Once you have collected those measurements and thoughts, the next step is to start thinking of alteration strategies. This chart should help you do that.

Measurement/ feature	Your own measurement or observation	Measurement for pattern size or flat pattern measurement for lengths	Difference to add or allow in alterations	Adjustment strategy*
Upper chest/bust and full bust			Are you larger or smaller than a B cup (the default) or the cup size specified by the pattern?	If not within the pattern bust range, do a full or small bust alteration (page 103). For minor additions, pivot the pattern out, up to ½˝ on each side seam.
Operational waist				Add to the side seam or increase by the pivot method (pages 96 and 106).
Widest lower body measurement				Add to the side seam or increase by the pivot method (pages 96 and 106).
Distance of widest measurement down from waist				Add width as above level with this depth measurement.
Back waist length				Add or subtract length as required by the slide method (page 106) or along pattern's marked lengthening or shortening line.
Arm length				Add or subtract length as required to the middle, along the sleeve marked lengthening or shortening line or by the slide method.
Bust depth				Move the end-point of the dart up or down as required or move the entire dart up or down by the block method (page 98).

Measurement/feature	Your own measurement or observation	Measurement for pattern size or flat pattern measurement for lengths	Difference to add or allow in alterations	Adjustment strategy*
Bust span				Move the end-point of the dart in or out, closer to the bust point (½″–1″), or reposition princess seams so they run directly over the bust point.
Upper arm / bicep width				Add or subtract width as required by either the seam or pivot-and-slide method (pages 98 and 106).
Shoulder length				Move the seamline at the end of the shoulder in or out as required and confirm the fit through the muslin method (page 93).
Back width				Back width requirements vary by pattern style as well as body dimension. Adjust through the muslin method (page 93).
Waist to knee				Change pants lengths by moving knee placement up and down through the slide method (page 106); also see Resources (page 251).
Calf width				Add width below the knee by even additions to the inseam and outseam, confirmed by the muslin method (page 93).
Shoulder slope	Determine if shoulders are more sloped or square than standard.	For minor tweaks, look for set-in sleeve patterns for square shoulders and raglan or dolman sleeve patterns for sloped shoulders. It is always easier to work with shapes like your own.		For adjustments of ½″ or more, adjust with the pivot method (page 106); also see Resources (page 251).
Neck angle		Patterns with back neck darts or princess seams		See muslin method (page 93), and create darts as required.
Lower body front and back dart length and placement	Decide if you need shaping between the waist and lower body and where.			In areas that need darts, lengthen or shorten darts by moving end points up and down as required. If darts need to be repositioned in the waist, move by the block method (page 98).

* Since it is easier/smarter to add than to subtract width from a pattern, most of the alterations here are for increases.

ASSESSING THE THIRD DIMENSION: CROTCH SHAPE

Once you have a sense of your body's realities and what pattern adjustments they might require, the next area you have to think about is crotch shape.

Understanding your crotch profile is so important to finding a pants pattern that fits. And finding a pants pattern that fits is truly the Holy Grail of sewing.

I personally know women who have been adjusting the same pants pattern for 30 years and are still not happy with the result—simply because they have never considered crotch shape. Don't let this be you, please don't let this be you.

I spoke in the last chapter about zeroing in on a pattern company that seems to work from a crotch shape like yours, but we need to be more specific about how you measure or more accurately assess that.

Crotch seams deal with the three-dimensionality of the body in a way that few other seams do. These seams, both the front and back crotch, bisect the figure and need to be evaluated this way.

Start with what you can see. Note the silhouette of your own particular curve, belly to backside. Where are you full and where are you flat? Where are you high and where are you low? Imagine the shape of the crotch seams that would mirror your particular shape and hold that thought.

Measuring Crotch Shape with a Flexible Ruler

If you find a simple visual check hard to do, there is a slightly more sophisticated approach you can take.

It will, however, require:

⊗ One of your belts

⊗ Flexible ruler

⊗ Paper

⊗ Ponytail elastic or rubber band

A 30″+ ruler is ideal, particularly if you are curvy, but these can be hard to come by unless you order one online. A number of sewing notion suppliers carry them. On the other hand, 24″ flexible rulers are widely available at any of the big box office supply stores, so that's what I have used here. Note that it is likely that the 24″ ruler might be an inch or two short front and back. To allow for that, be prepared to measure that little extra from the end of the ruler to your waist and add it to your calculations. This won't be necessary if you are working with a 30″ ruler.

1. Put on a pair of closely fitted pants you feel comfortable in—leggings are great. Put on the belt and settle it where it feels comfortable on your waist. Many folks recommend using a length of elastic to mark a waistline, but I prefer to use a thin leather belt. Belts tend to stay put and feel more accurately like a waistband. The bottom of the belt fairly accurately represents any waistline stitching line.

2. Slide the ponytail elastic onto the 12″ mark on the ruler (or the 15″ mark for a 30″ ruler). You are not going to be able to read this ruler when it is between your legs, so it is nice to make the midpoint something you can feel.

3. Next situate the ruler between your legs with the marked center around where you think your crotch seams would intersect.

4. Mold the ruler around your body, pressing it gently to follow your curves. Keep it comfortable. What's interesting about pants and crotch seams is that they actually fit close to the body. As a result, it is possible to create a mirror image with this method that is a surprisingly accurate representation of the crotch curve you will need. Note the distance that may exist between the end of the ruler and the bottom of the belt.

5. Step out of the ruler, being careful to preserve its shape.

6. Lay the ruler on a piece of paper. Trace around the inside of the ruler, marking the front and back waistline and the center of your crotch. Add to either end of the crotch length as required to measure up to the bottom of the waist/belt. For example, when I used the 24″ ruler for my own shape, I added 3⅜″ to the back crotch and 1″ to the front.

You now have a very useful template that will be an enormous help for your pant fitting. The template can be used for both for identifying patterns that might fit you and a basis for redrafting any crotch seams for your own shape.

In Chapter 5: Altering a Flat Pattern to Fit (page 84), we will look at the pattern adjustment needed for extra tummy room, obvious when you look at my own belly curve (below) as an example of how the crotch curve template can be used.

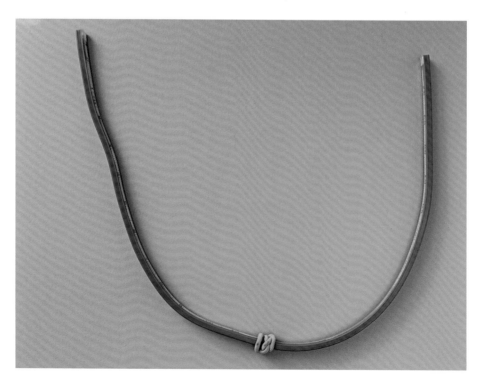

MEASURING CHILDREN

I was once trapped alone with a whole birthday party's worth of preschoolers in a restaurant. I ran through my full repertoire of interesting activities and finally resorted to the only prop I had left—the measuring tape I always carry in my purse. A riveting game of "let's measure everyone's head" turned into an interesting research experience.

I discovered that most people under or around the age of five have a head measurement, waist measurement, hip measurement, and inseam measurement more or less the same number.

This is handy information to have if you ever have to measure a small sleeping child. As long as you can reach a limb, you can figure out the rest yourself.

Note, too, that kids grow in limb's lengths before they get wider. Be wary of moving up in pattern sizes just because your child is older. You may find all you have to do to make an existing pattern fit is to add length to bodies, pants legs, and sleeves. I once made pajamas for my three children ages four, six, and nine all from a size 4 pattern, adding only length for each older child. Nice to be able to sew.

Barbara's Tips

✓ Choosing Pattern Sizes

Don't pay much attention to the actual *numbers* when choosing a pattern size. Sewing pattern sizes bear little relationship to ready-to-wear sizes. It is common for a retail size 12 to fit a size 18 or larger in patterns, so don't panic. This seems to be particularly true in the way the major pattern companies determine sizes. Many indie patterns seem to have sizes that are a closer match to those found in retail clothing, and some even use letters instead of numbers to avoid the issue altogether.

✓ Measuring Pants Length

Because crotch depth can vary so much by pant style—jeans are cut closer to the body and tailored pants much lower—the most reliable finished pant length measurement to take is along the side seam not along the inseam.

✓ Jacket Sleeve Length

Figuring out how long to make jacket sleeves can be tricky. The best advice is to place the palm of your hand flat on a table and then measure from your shoulder point to the table's surface. I would make a coat sleeve, which may have to cover a jacket, about ¾″ longer than this.

✓ Different Hip Heights

Older women who have carried many children on their hips typically have one hip, the child side, higher than the other. If this might be the case, take 2 hip-depth measurements, one for each side, and adjust skirt and pants lengths accordingly.

✓ Another Useful Arm Measurement

With shoulder seam placement so dependent on style—drop sleeves are an example—it can be useful to take a neckline-to-wrist measurement as a benchmark.

✓ When to Use Multisize Patterns

Multisize patterns can be helpful if your measurements are only a size apart in different areas. However, trying to blend in the cutting lines for more than one size can leave you with unnatural looking curves. Using the measurement advice in this chapter and the flat pattern alteration ideas in the next will help you achieve a smoother, more personalized fit.

5
Altering a
Flat Pattern to Fit

WE ALL KNOW THE FEELING OF VULNERABILITY THAT COMES WITH WEARING SOMETHING LESS THAN WELL-FITTING and we fear shows off the worst of our bodies. Learning to fit changes all that. Getting to know your own shape well—something fitting requires—leads you to an appreciation of your own body. Fit is about self-respect. When you wear something made for your own body and to your own taste, you step out with confidence and pride that comes from knowing you did this with your own hands and your own skill. There is real power in learning how to alter your own patterns to fit.

Of course, fitting takes skill. It takes practice and patience. At times, it also takes perseverance and always requires optimism.

But the process of learning to fit is worth it, because the product—a garment that fits— is what you deserve.

WHY LEARN TO ALTER A FLAT PATTERN?

There are two reasons most of us make changes to a paper pattern.

First, we need to adjust the pattern to head off fitting issues we can see coming a mile away. For example, if we have a waist 3″ larger than the pattern calls for, we can deal with it before we cut.

Second, once we have seen the pattern in fabric, either in a trial "muslin" (page 93) or in an actual sewn project, we can see changes we know for sure we want to make the next time we use this same pattern. We want to lower that bust dart or make the neckline a little higher, for example. Transferring these changes to the pattern paper means that next time out we can just sew up the same pattern "without thinking," which in sewist-speak means without the need to fiddle with fitting again.

In both cases, these changes to the paper pattern move the sewist closer to what all sewists want most—a repertoire of elusive "tried 'n' true" patterns (TNTs). Once we have patterns we can trust, we can use them again and again in many variations without stress. We can even use them as the basis for altering another pattern to fit.

1960s-style dress; multiple seamlines, all ending at center front under the bust; an easy pattern to fit

More complicated than it looks

Angled seams act like darts for shaping.

HOW TO KNOW IF A PATTERN NEEDS YOUR HELP

There are some pretty clear principles to help identify and resolve fitting issues well and a variety of ways to transfer these changes to paper. Let's start with how you identify the pattern changes you might need to make.

Listen to the Messages

All day long your clothes are talking to you about fit.

A skirt or blouse that rides up in a tight area is trying to find a smaller place to settle—a too small hip area moving up to the waist, for example. A back waistband that slides down when you bend over means the back crotch measurement is too short.

Read the Folds

Folds indicate too much fabric. A fold of fabric at the top of a pair of pants under the seat might mean the back crotch seam is too high and needs to lowered, in essence shifting that space from the fabric to your body. A fold at the center front of a scoop neckline means more fabric there than is needed for a narrow chest, and it should be eliminated, usually by patting out that excess to the nearest seams, in this case the shoulder seams.

Follow the Wrinkles

Wrinkles on the other hand, indicate not enough fabric in an area and even more usefully actually point, like arrows, to where extra fabric is needed. Wrinkles that directly zero in on the full part of the bust are a clear indication that a full bust alteration is needed.

Don't Take Your Eyes Off the Grain

Grain tells you everything. Garments are cut so the strongest grain, the lengthwise, runs up and down the body. When a garment doesn't fit, the first thing to move off-kilter is grain. Follow the grainline and it will lead you back to the source of the problem. Off grain is seen most often in details that require some hang, such as a pant leg or sleeve. To correct fit in these areas, don't try to add or subtract fabric. Instead, realign the garment section from the top. This is where it helps if you have made a muslin test garment first.

To correct the hang of a sleeve from a shoulder, rotate the sleeve in the armhole until the straight of grain hangs directly from the end of the individual's shoulder point. It doesn't matter if the large dot at the top of the sleeve is moved away from the shoulder seam—what does matter is that you have corrected the grain and therefore the fit.

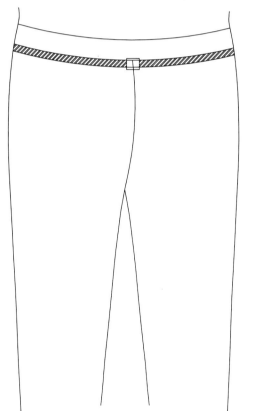

To correct the hang of a skirt or pair of pants, put on the same thin belt you used to mark your waist when taking a crotch measurement with a flexible ruler (page 79). Using the bottom of the belt as a tool to establish the waistline seam, realign the garment until it hangs properly, pulling some sections higher under the belt and some lower. The vertical grain of the garment should hang straight and perpendicular to the ground. At this point, draw a chalk line along the bottom of the belt—this will be your new waistline stitching line— and trim all fabric a seam-allowance distance above that new stitching line. Make sense?

In this example, this full abdomen needs more fabric at the center of the waist. Pull that extra fabric below the belt, mark the new waist stitching line at the bottom of the belt, and trim.

THE FIRST PRINCIPLES OF PATTERN ALTERATION

There are a number of different ways you can alter a paper pattern to fit. In my opinion each method has its own strengths. My own alteration approach uses different approaches for different situations and that seems to work well. However, you may find one particular system seems to make most sense to you. In that case, focus on that one method and learn more by accessing the resources listed at the end of this book (page 251).

If the thought of pattern adjustments overwhelms you, don't let it. This is easier than you think. There is a definite and same work order to the process, *whatever approach you use*, and if you follow this order you should be fine.

Do Length Changes First

Your height and things like arm and leg length are pretty fixed. This makes changes to these areas of a pattern a safe and logical place to start. To help you identify what might need to be adjusted, compare your own vertical length measurements directly to the pattern. Too easy.

We have talked about measurements more fully in Chapter 4: If It Fits, They Will Wear It (page 60). Now is the time to refer to those measurements and compare them to the pattern.

You should check these measurements:

⊗ Back length, nape of neck to waist

⊗ Front lengths, neck edge to bust apex (a.k.a. nipple) and bust apex to waist

⊗ Apex to apex (important for situating vertical princess seams that should run right over the fullest part of the bust)

⊗ Arm length and shoulder point to the hem of your favorite sleeves are useful, too.

⊗ Waist to the fullest part of the lower body. Check this at the side seam. Remember that the fullest part is highly variable on different figures—belly, high hip, hip over the seat, or top of the legs. You will have recorded this. Just find the same spot on the pattern and measure from there.

⊗ Waist to knee. Obviously helpful for knee-length skirts but also useful for adjusting pants lengths and shapes (page 72).

⊗ Ideal top lengths. Know your most flattering top and jacket lengths and check those against all new patterns.

Do Width Changes Next

Note that you should add width to the outer seams of patterns and not to the interior. There are several ways to do this—by simple side-seam additions, by pivoting the pattern, and by the seam method, all described later in this chapter.

On to the Third Dimension

After you have made any changes necessary to length and then width, move on to the three B's (bust, belly, and butt) and to the two places where garments travel right through from front to back: armholes and crotches. Since none of us are paper dolls, these are the areas where the most perplexing fitting challenges lie.

You may need to call on more than one fitting approach to deal with each of them. The alteration ideas in this chapter will help you get started. You also can check out the fitting resources (page 251) for detailed solutions to different fitting issues. Look for the title that develops the fitting approach that feels most natural to you first.

Do One Adjustment at a Time

A change in one area of a garment can eliminate the need for pattern adjustments in another. For example, removing the front darts in a skirt can make wrinkles over the belly disappear, when simply shortening the darts isn't enough. However, removing darts can also have the effect of making the waist wider. Think whether you need that, too.

On the other hand, a single adjustment also can create a new problem elsewhere. Scooping out a back crotch, as often suggested for a full backside, can then make the side seams too tight, and you will then have to make a new adjustment for that.

Slow down and take it one change at a time. Having multiple alterations implemented all at once just makes it that much harder to trace back to the real problem and fix it.

Also, give alterations time. Make a muslin (page 93) and wear it awhile. Wearing it often will bring additional fitting areas to the surface. A waistband that is too tight when you sit at work all day, a neck that rides up, or a back that doesn't give you enough reaching room all need to be considered. I usually fine-tune my pattern adjustments again at this stage and make any changes necessary to the paper pattern before I sign off on it.

Know When to Stop

Don't fit past the point of comfort or flattery. Over-fitting can eliminate wearing ease (it fits but you can't move) or design ease (it might fit, but the sheath now looks like a caftan). Also be aware that fitting too closely can overarticulate parts of your body—a belly like mine, for example, is better left skimmed.

DIFFERENT WAYS OF ALTERING A PATTERN

With the overall principles of flat pattern alteration in mind, your next job is to decide what alteration method will be most helpful for the issue you need to adjust. Here is the menu.

Approach 1: The Muslin Method

Making and adjusting a trial garment before you tackle your fashion fabric is really the gold standard of fitting. Nothing ever behaves like fabric but fabric, and having the opportunity to fine-tune a pattern in the real thing is the best way to adjust any pattern. It is a method I always use when the stakes are high, when sewing something particularly fitted, or to be made in expensive fabric.

A muslin trial garment, also called a *toile*, can let you do so much. In addition to making the necessary changes to width and length very obvious, a muslin also gives you a chance to play around with and adjust the more three-dimensional aspects of garment fitting, such as darts and princess seams. With your eyes and your hands, these shaping elements of construction can be reshaped and repositioned, added where needed or even removed until the fit is perfect. Working with a muslin, you can pinch in excesses, take up folds, and let out seams. You can even sew in extensions where necessary to add width and length. Fitting in fabric also gives you a chance to correct grain where you need to—rehanging a sleeve so it hangs straight on a rounded shoulder, for example, or adjusting the waistline of a pair of pants, moving it up and down around the wearer's body until the legs hang properly.

FITTING WITH A MUSLIN

Muslin fitting is always interesting and tells you so much about how a final garment might fit. The muslin can be either a basic shape-fitting pattern for general fit information and strategies or a trial version of a specific pattern you want to test. In either case, using the muslin to fit is not difficult. Just work methodically.

1. Use a muslin or any stable-grain fabric for your fitting garment and draw a straight-of-grain line on the fabric with a fine marker so it is easy to see. So many fitting issues can be identified and resolved by following the path the grain takes.

2. Cut out the pattern with larger, say 1″ seam allowances. This will give you room to let seams out if needed when you fit. Don't cut out the facings and collars yet; wait until you see if they need to be fitted to match your changes in the main garment pieces.

3. Mark the pieces with key information. I use fine-tip markers, as radical as that may seem. I draw on waist and bust levels, hip depth, and the high and low points of the lower body contours (the fullest part front and back) to help double-check dart placement and length. I also label each pattern piece, mark all dots—such as the one at the top of the sleeve—and write "left" and "right" and any other useful identifying information.

4. Construct the entire garment as you would the finished product, but with a machine basting stitch. Rather than backstitching at the beginning and end of every seam, leave long thread tails so the seams don't start opening during fitting but will still be easy to take out.

In most cases it is not necessary to sew on facings and collars, unless these are distinct and need fitting. But you should set in the sleeves, baste up the hems, and install zippers. Since zippers are put into seams that may need to be adjusted themselves, I usually baste the zippers in by hand because that makes them easier to remove if necessary.

5. Staystitch around necklines and sleeve-less armholes so you can see if changes need to be made at stitching lines. Clip these openings, too, so they lie flat during fitting.

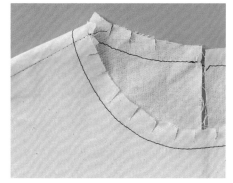

6. Try on the muslin. Wear it around for a while, sitting and doing other activities that you would do in the final garment. Take note of where changes need to be made, letting out or taking in seams and adding extensions, if necessary.

Count on at least three fittings when working with a muslin. Since a tweak in one area can change the fit in another area, take time to get all these issues worked through.

TRANSFERRING THE MUSLIN INFORMATION TO THE FLAT PATTERN

Once the muslin has been fitted to your satisfaction, the next step is to take it apart and transfer all the changes and information back onto paper to alter the pattern. The easiest way to do this is to carefully clip the muslin seams open, press the pieces flat, and then trim off all seam allowances right to the final stitching line. This last step will allow you to see the pattern changes more clearly; you can add the appropriate seam allowance later. The muslin pieces can then be traced onto paper and these tracings used to make the appropriate changes to the original pattern. I always find it easiest to transfer changes when working paper to paper.

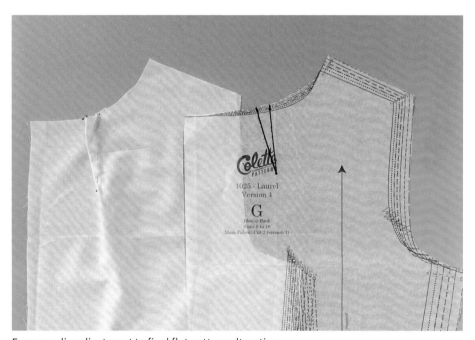

From muslin adjustment to final flat pattern alteration

Approach 2: The Simple Side-Seam Additions Method

Of course, not all flat-pattern alterations need the work of a muslin. Many of the more common adjustments can be made directly to the pattern pieces based on discrepancies between body and pattern-size measurement. The most basic way this is often done is by minor adjustments to the side seams.

Multisize patterns make this easy, offering the opportunity to cut size 10 shoulders, size 12 waist, and size 14 hips. Single-size patterns, however, will require you to make your own additions.

Make sure that you make all changes to the side or the side front seams, never along the center front or center back. Alterations to the center of garments, crotch seams excepted, are a tricky business and should be avoided. Wiggling around a pattern on the center front fold, for example, can quickly move things off grain and is nothing but a recipe for wonkiness.

MAKING SIDE-SEAM ADDITIONS

The guidelines for accurate simple additions to the side seams of a pattern piece are pretty straightforward.

Calculate the amount you need to add and divide it by the number of seams in question. In a skirt with a simple front and back, that would be 4 side-seam allowances: 2 at the front and 2 at the back.

As an example, to accommodate a waist that is 4″ wider than the pattern, you would then add 1″ to each side seam for a total overall addition of 4″. Taper the addition down to the widest part of the lower body.

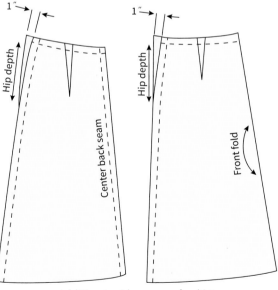

Addition to side seams of a skirt

Of course, the more seams you have in which to make the additions, the more gracefully this can be done. A 4½″ addition divided by the 12 seam allowances of a 6-panel skirt, for example, would require only ⅜″ to be added to each seam—quite a difference and barely noticeable.

Remember, too, that once a seam has been moved out, it shouldn't be moved back in further down. This is really important when adding extra to a hip area if you want to avoid a hip cupping, jodhpur-style look to skirts or pants. Once made, any additions are wisely continued right down to the hem. Of course, when you make a straight skirt, you have the option to "peg" the skirt in a bit for shape, but do this only by a few inches and only in the side seam near the hem.

Also keep in mind that if you increase in an area that has a connecting piece, be sure you make a similar increase in the connecting piece so they will still fit together. I know this sounds obvious, but it's easy to forget. For example, if you add to the side seams of T-shirt for bust/back ease, which increases the underarm area, make sure you also make the same addition to the seams of the sleeve. Here is what that looks like.

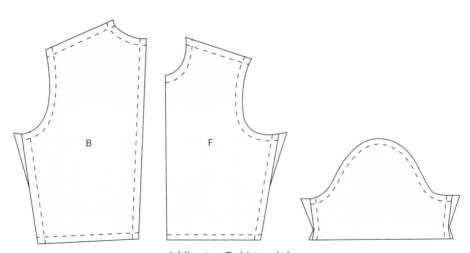

Adding to a T-shirt and sleeve

Approach 3: The Block Method

Even more complex pattern alterations don't have to be difficult. An example of this is the block method, in which you can reposition shaping details and seams by simply cutting around them and moving them over, up, or down.

USING THE BLOCK METHOD

I always enjoy using the block method—it is so easy. One way I use it is to raise or lower bust darts. A lower bust than the pattern allows is a common problem, particularly for larger cup sizes or more mature figures. To lower a dart, it is possible to just move the end point of the dart down, of course, but this tends to change the shape of the dart entirely and may affect the design. Far simpler I feel is to simply cut a box around the entire dart and move it down the required distance. Here is what that looks like.

The block method is also a wonderful solution to a fitting problem many sewists have with pants: the horizontal folds that appear under the seat at the top of the legs.

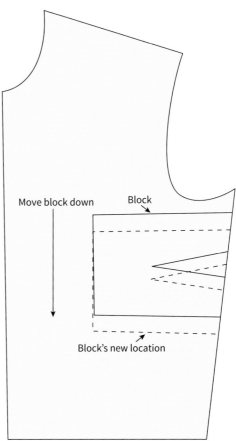

Move block down

Block

Block's new location

Many strategies can fix this issue. But in my experience, these folds are most often caused (counterintuitively) by a dropped or low seat, a common figure development as we get older. In this situation, the curve of the back crotch seam cuts into the body too high for the realities of that particular body and needs to be lowered an amount equal to the depth of the observed folds—in essence, moving that extra space from the fabric back to the body. Again, the fix can be made by just cutting out a block, in this case from mid-center back crotch to a point about 3″ down the back inseam; sliding it the whole unit down; and truing the seams as necessary.

Note: If you shorten the back inseam, you will need to shorten the front inseam by the same amount so the two seams still match.

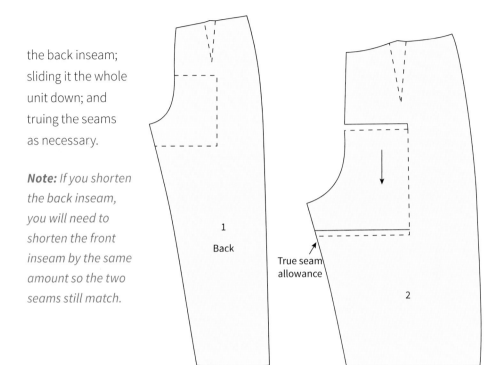

This back-crotch block can be shifted around to address a number of other back fitting issues, too. Here it has been moved out horizontally to add width across the back and down, too, to add to the length of the back-crotch seam to allow for a curvy rear.

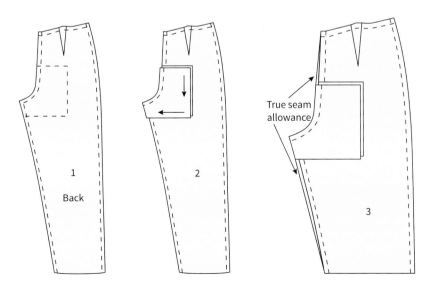

Moving the block in, in the opposite direction, adjusts the pattern for a flatter seat and at the same time thinner thighs.

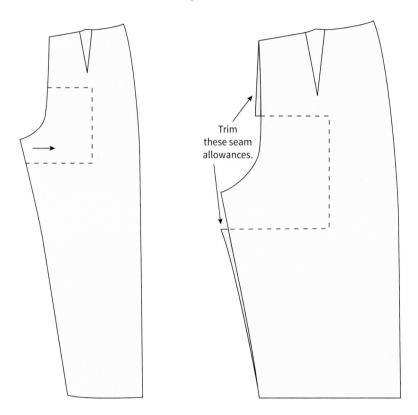

Trim these seam allowances.

Notice that one of the beauties of the block system is that only the area that needs adjustment is touched.

In the full and flat seat adjustments, the above-the-waist dimension and side seams are unchanged. In all cases, of course, the stitching lines will need to be redrawn as required to meet the new location of the crotch curves.

Approach 4: The Slash-and-Spread Method

The block method of relocating contour features might remind you of the slash-and-spread methods you have seen in books and online, where the pattern is cut apart and pieces moved. It actually is quite different.

The classic slash-and-spread method does more than cut out and move pattern blocks. Traditionally done, slash-and-spread involves cutting into the pattern piece at points of adjustment, usually stopping just short of the edge of the paper to maintain a "hinge," and pulling the paper apart to insert additions or overlapping it to make an area smaller. Except in a few special circumstances this method of pattern alteration is not my favorite approach. Why?

⊛ Cutting up the pattern and moving it around so easily can move important structural elements off grain. This just can't be allowed to happen. Straight grain carries the weight of the garment; if this gets shifted, the hang of the entire garment takes on a mind of its own. The best alteration methods maintain grain and work around it.

⊛ Unless you are diligent and carefully trace duplicate pattern pieces for slashing and spreading, you risk permanently destroying the original pattern. You are going to want to get that original back if the garment needs further adjustment.

⊛ The directions for using this method most often show diagrams of where to cut and where to spread or overlap the pattern, but they don't give you guidelines of *exactly* where to cut or *exactly* how to figure out how much to spread or overlap. This can be very confusing for new sewists.

● This method often creates more than one adjustment at the same time, and some of these may be unintended. For example, L-shaped cuts, such as those that go across a hip and up to a waistline, can have a ricochet effect—bagging under the belly, for example—and can produce new problems elsewhere but leave few hints of where to source or how to fix them.

● Significant changes to the interior of the garment piece, something that can happen when using slash-and-spread, can really change the shape of the side seams. The usual instruction is to "true" or blend in those seams; but when the change has been major, this can be really hard to do smoothly.

For these reasons, I tend to use other methods to alter my own patterns. My exception is for the enlargement of a bust dart. I think why slash-and-spread works so well for darts is that the reference points for the cuts are so discernable—the center of the dart and the front notch on the armhole—which keeps it all under control.

MINI LESSON

Making a Full Bust Alteration

To make more room for the bust in a top with darts, a classic slash-and-spread Full Bust Alteration (FBA) works well. Since this technique does not change neckline or armhole shapes, it is an excellent way to increase for bust measurement in a pattern that has been selected to fit proportionally smaller shoulders and upper bust. It is also a great way to increase the cup size and dart area for a bust larger than the standard B cup pattern draft.

1. Make the first cut. Slash the pattern piece through the middle of the bust dart and past the end of the dart. Stop short of the apex (which should be 1″–2″ past the end of the dart) by just a shade to save some paper as a "hinge" pivot point later on.

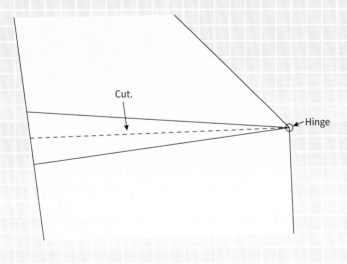

2. Make the second cut. Cut up straight from the bottom of the garment, parallel to center front up to the apex, taking great care not to cut into the first cut. Again, you are going to need that sliver of paper. At the apex, change the angle of the cut and continue cutting up to the front armhole notch, a point about one-third of the way up the armhole seam. Stop just short of cutting right all the way through the paper to make another hinge pivot point. These little paper hinges will keep the pattern intact when it is spread.

3. Spread the pattern right over the fullest part of the bust by half the over-all amount you need to add to the bust. For example, to increase the bust area from a 36″ draft to fit a 38″ bust, spread the paper at the apex by 1″, which multiplied by 2 sides = 38″. Rearrange the other cut edges so the pattern lies flat. You will find you will have to open and enlarge the dart to do this.

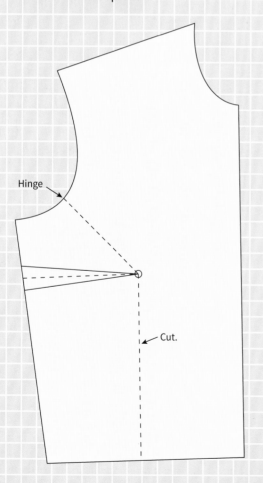

Hinge

Cut.

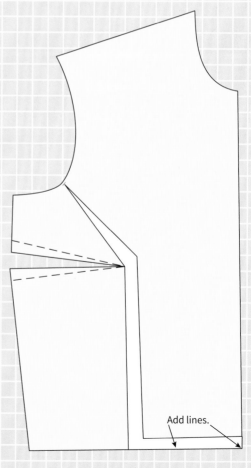

Add lines.

4. Add to the length as required to even out the hem of the garment. Opening the pattern at the bust and dart naturally also adds width above the bust up to the armhole as well as both width and length to the top below the bust. This is helpful. However, don't forget that a fuller bust consumes extra fabric both above the bust and in length, and it is important to remember to accommodate the need for extra length, too.

If you need to then adjust further for a smaller midriff and waist, relative to the full bust, you could reduce the extra width in the torso with the addition of waist-to-bust darts. Just pinch out the excess fabric, muslin-fitting style, to see how long and how deep you might want these darts to be. Just be careful, if you add darts below the bust, to keep them on grain and parallel to center front so they won't twist.

To make a Small Bust Alteration (SBA), follow the steps on the previous page, but instead of spreading the slashed pattern, overlap it as required.

TIP To keep your pattern from falling apart, insert paper under the spaces created when the pattern is spread. To keep this neat, it is helpful to work with the slashed pattern over a sheet of paper. This way changes can be taped in place as you go. At the end of the process you will have a nice new permanent pattern piece.

Approach 5: The Pivot-and-Slide Method

Pivot-and-slide is an eccentric, or at least very original, approach to flat pattern alteration. It is also fast and helpful for many fitting challenges. The concept was made popular in the early 1980s by the Sew/Fit Company and since been promoted by the fabulous Nancy Zieman (see Resources, page 251).

"Pivot" and "slide" are actually two different techniques: *sliding*, a method for adding length, and *pivoting*, a method for adding width. Both methods keep the original paper pattern intact. Each method can be used either right on the fabric, where adjustments are marked and cut in directly or on paper to generate a completely new adjusted version of the pattern.

SLIDING A PATTERN TO ADD LENGTH

As a tall person, I have been adding length to patterns my whole life, and I know the pitfalls. Simply adding or subtracting inches at the bottom of pattern pieces can distort shape. Just think of how adding 3˝ to the bottom of an A-line skirt can extend it into a giant triangle with pointy sides. Sliding the pattern up and down to change length is a much better way to preserve design lines and is so easy to do.

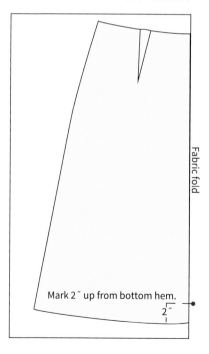

Here is how to add 2˝ in length to a skirt, working directly on the fabric at the pattern layout stage.

1. Pin the pattern to the fabric, leaving enough extra fabric at the top of the garment to accommodate the amount of length you want to add. For example, if you want to add 2˝, leave at least 2˝ between the end of the fabric and the top of the pattern. Place a pin or make a chalk mark next to the fold line or center back seam, 2˝ above the hemline.

Mark 2˝ up from bottom hem.

2˝

Fabric fold

2. Start cutting out, but cut *only* along the hemline/bottom of the pattern piece and about only 1˝ or so *up* the side seams. Unpin the pattern (this is the eccentric part) and slide the pattern piece up—*straight up*—so the bottom of the pattern is now right beside the pin or 2˝ mark. Repin the pattern in this position. Depending on the shape of the side seam, you might have to fold under a bit of excess tissue as necessary to continue the smooth line of the seam as you complete cutting out the garment.

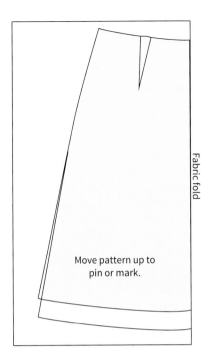

Move pattern up to pin or mark.

Fabric fold

SLIDING A PATTERN TO SHORTEN

The steps are the similar to those for length, except the pattern is slid down below the cut hem line and not above it. Here is how to slide a pattern to shorten, in this case by 2˝ working directly on the fabric.

1. Make a mark *on the pattern* 2˝ above the bottom of the pattern piece. Pin the pattern to the fabric.

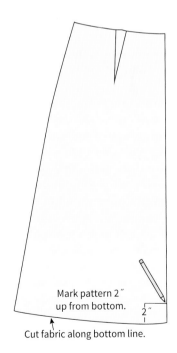

Mark pattern 2˝ up from bottom.

2˝

Cut fabric along bottom line.

2. Cut out the hemline/bottom of the pattern piece *only*. Do not cut up any of the side seam at all. Unpin the pattern and slide the pattern piece *down* so the bottom of the cut hem is even with the 2″ mark on the pattern. Cut out the remainder of the garment, truing the side seams as required.

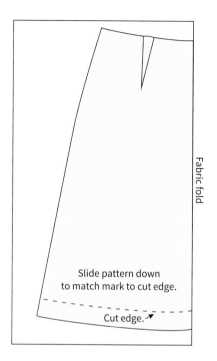

Fabric fold

Slide pattern down to match mark to cut edge.

Cut edge.

PIVOTING A PATTERN TO ADD WIDTH

Sliding a pattern is an easy way to add or subtract length. Width can be added or subtracted to specific pattern areas by pivoting the pattern around an impaled pin, another eccentric but effective technique. Pattern pivoting is useful because it focuses the alterations on the areas that need them while still preserving the existing shape of seams, necklines, and armholes. Many other systems, such as simple changes to side seams, are not able to do this.

PIVOTING A PATTERN TO ADD WIDTH TO A T-SHIRT BUST

Unlike the Full Bust Alteration (page 103), which adds bust space to a garment with a dart, this method adds bust width to a garment, such as a T-shirt, without a dart. As an example, it also gives you an idea how pattern pivoting works.

1. Determine how much extra fabric you need across the bust. This can be done by comparing your personal measurement to that given for the pattern size or by comparing your cup size to the pattern's standard B cup. Add a total ½″ for each cup size larger than a B for each side or 1″ overall. For this example, I am adding 1½″ to the bust line. Divided by 2 means an addition of ¾″ on each side at bust level to the front. Note that all additions are made to the front pattern piece only.

2. Pin the front pattern piece to the fabric and make a mark or put a pin in the fabric ¾″ out from the side seam at bust level, at the fullest part of the bust, which usually is more or less where the armhole meets the side seam.

3. Start cutting out the pattern. Starting at the center fold at the front neck edge, cut up to and down the shoulder. Stop cutting at the end of the shoulder at the armhole edge. *Do not cut out the armhole yet.*

4. Now stab a pin into the point/dot where the shoulder seam and the top armhole seams intersect. Unpin the rest of the pattern from the fabric and, using the pin at the shoulder/armhole as an anchor, swivel the pattern piece out so the side seam now touches the pin placed at the ¾″ mark. Cut out the armhole in this new pattern position, *but do not cut out the side seam yet*.

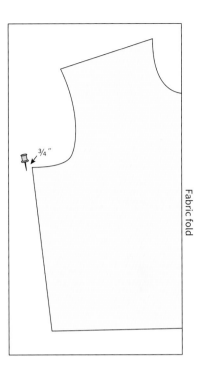

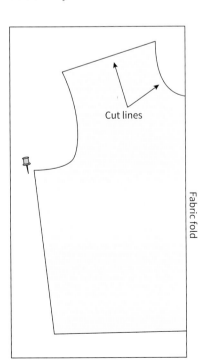

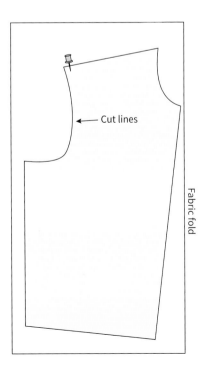

5. Remove the pivot pin from the shoulder/armhole intersection and reposition it at the point where the side seam and armhole intersect. Again, use the pin as an anchor to swivel the pattern piece back, moving the full pattern piece so it is again parallel to the fold, reestablishing the straight of grain. Some folks pivot the bottom side seam back to the fold, but as this distorts the grain of the side seams, I don't do that. Note that at this point the entire pattern piece will be an even distance from the fold, but not to worry. Just cut out the side seam and bottom of the top. Note the difference (at right) in the cutting lines (broken lines) and the pattern piece (solid lines).

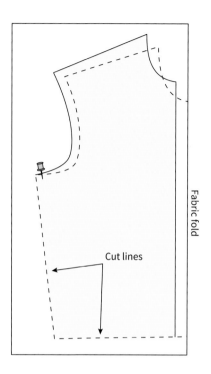

Fabric fold

Cut lines

Alteration done. This can of course all be done over a sheet of paper rather than directly onto the fabric, in which case you have made a new altered permanent pattern piece.

Notice in this method, the shape of the original armhole has been retained; there is no need to make any changes to the sleeve width to fit.

Approach 6: The Seam Method

All the previously explained alteration approaches can be used to make reliable changes to the width or length of garments or to reposition or fine-tune fitting details. To my mind, this leaves one major challenge—how to make significant adjustments along the internal seamlines without distorting them, without moving the garment off-grain, and without creating new problems elsewhere in the garment. The seam method addresses this problem directly and effectively.

The seam method was developed and popularized by Judith Rasband. It is quite unique. In this system, the pattern's *seam allowances* are cut free at the stitching line and hinged at each end of the alteration area or along curves, and they can be pulled out or moved in to add or subtract fabric from a specific area. The beauty of this method is that it allows the sewist to make changes as required to the pattern without having to "true," or blend in, the seams; to maintain the shape of the original pattern; and to adjust only along the areas requiring alteration. The seam method is useful when working with shaped areas, such as princess seams, or when changes need to be made to a specific body area, such as the abdomen.

For two examples of how I interpret the seam method in my own sewing for pattern alterations, see Adding to the Bust in a Princess Seam (below) and Adding for a Full Abdomen in Pants (page 113). (For other alterations using this method, see Judith Rasband's many publications on fitting. For example, to see how she uses it to address back crotch fitting issues, go to threadsmagazine.com > search 5053 > click Alter Patterns Using the Seam Method.)

ADDING TO THE BUST IN A PRINCESS SEAM

In this example, 1½˝ is added overall to the bust. Since a princess seam dress or top has 4 seam allowances, ⅜˝ needs to be added to each one. The side panel of a dress is illustrated.

1. Identify the area of the seam that needs the adjustment. In a princess seam this will be clearly in the area of the bust curve. Cut right through the seam allowance at the high point of the bust so the seam can be lengthened. Note that whenever a curve is increased, its seam length is increased too, so it is necessary to allow for that spread by cutting right across the seam allowance.

2. Cut along the stitching line only in the area to be adjusted. At each end of this area, cut out directly through the seam allowance, stopping just short of cutting right through and leaving a sliver of paper that creates a small "hinge" to keep the seam allowance attached to the pattern.

3. Pull the seam allowance away from the pattern to make the addition, in this case to add ⅜″ to the fullest part of the bust. Notice how doing this has also added fabric to the length of the seam to go over the bust, which is useful.

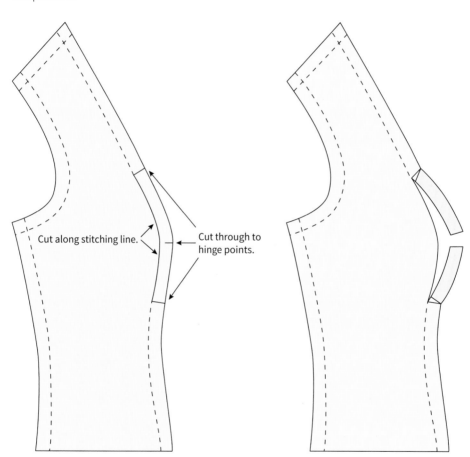

Cut along stitching line.

Cut through to hinge points.

4. Repeat this process in the bust area of the center front panel princess seams.

ADDING FOR A FULL ABDOMEN IN PANTS

In the Chapter 4: If It Fits, They Will Wear It (page 60), we talked about how to use a flexible ruler to make a personal crotch curve template. My own looks like this:

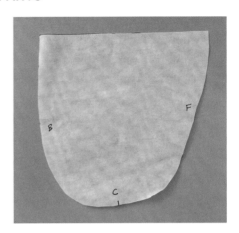

Looking at this shape, it is apparent that length needs to be added to the front crotch seam and width, too, at a specific area in the crotch curve. This is how you would do each of those pattern changes. Lay the front pants pattern pieces over paper so you can tape your changes in place.

To add length to the front crotch seam:

1. Start cutting right through the seam allowance at the point where the front crotch seam and waistline seams intersect. This cut will allow you to raise the seam to add length to the center front. Cut carefully along the waistline stitching. Stop just short of the side seam to maintain a tiny paper hinge.

2. Pull the cut seam allowance free and up to add as required.

To add width to the center crotch seam:

1. Based on your body shape, determine where the alteration needs to start down along the front crotch seam. This will be the lower hinge location. Mark it.

2. Cut along the center front stitching line, stopping at the marked lower hinge location and then out through the seam allowance again, stopping short to keep a paper hinge.

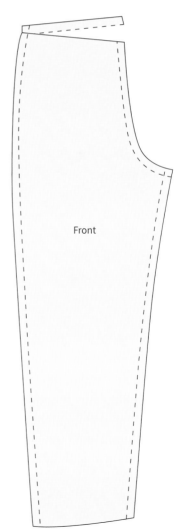

Front

3. Pull the front crotch seam allowances away from the pattern as necessary to match your own front crotch shape and undoubtedly a wider front waist measurement, too.

A pattern altered this way can, of course, be used to add both length and width to the front crotch, a common full abdomen alteration.

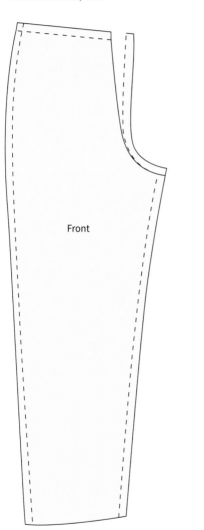

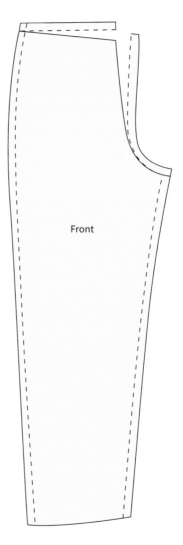

Front

Front

Now isn't that slick? And isn't pattern alteration easier than you thought it would be?

Barbara's Tips

✓ Be Prepared

Have a list handy of standard preferred finished measurements; skirt, pant, and sleeve lengths; and your most flattering top and jacket lengths for fast checks of vertical pattern measurements.

✓ Quick Fittings

Use facings as mini muslins. Cut and sew up neckline and armhole facings and try them on before you cut out a whole garment. How the facings fit will tell you what adjustments you might have to make.

✓ Don't Do This

Some patterns suggest you pin together paper pattern pieces to test the fit. I don't do this. Paper just never behaves like fabric, and envisioning a whole garment from half-pieces is pretty difficult.

✓ More Resources

For more complete descriptions of how to use any of these alteration methods, see Resources (page 251).

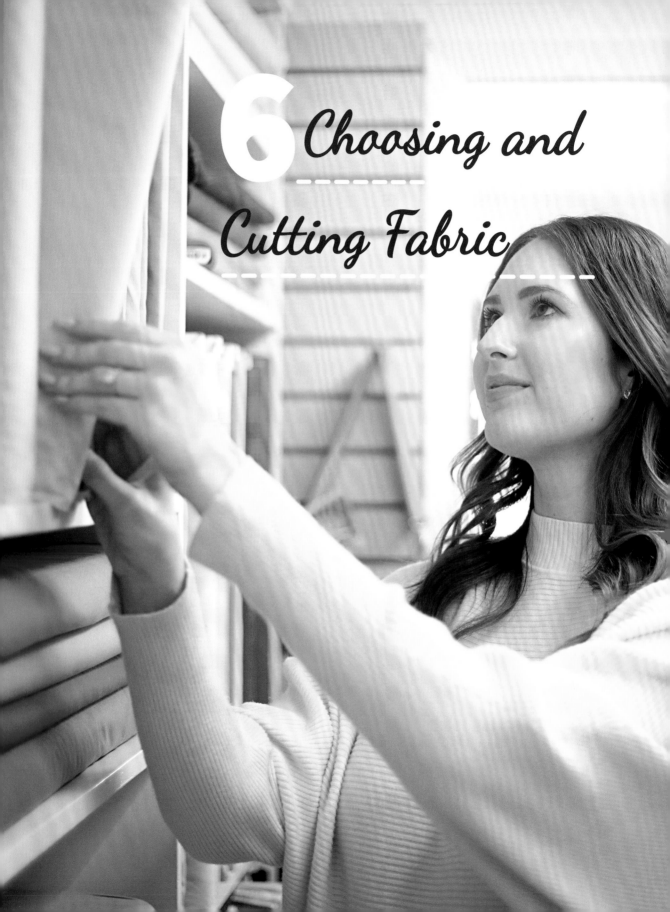

6 Choosing and Cutting Fabric

EVERY NEW SEWIST WANTS TO KNOW—WHAT FABRIC GOES WITH WHAT PATTERN?
Here's my advice. The best fabric choice decisions are made not only with your eyes, but also with your hands. Notice fabric people regularly talk about "hand." It matters. The fabric already knows what it wants to be. Touch will help you read those messages and apply them to your pattern.

Sometimes simple is best. In this dress, the linen does all the talking.

Let the fabric speak for itself.

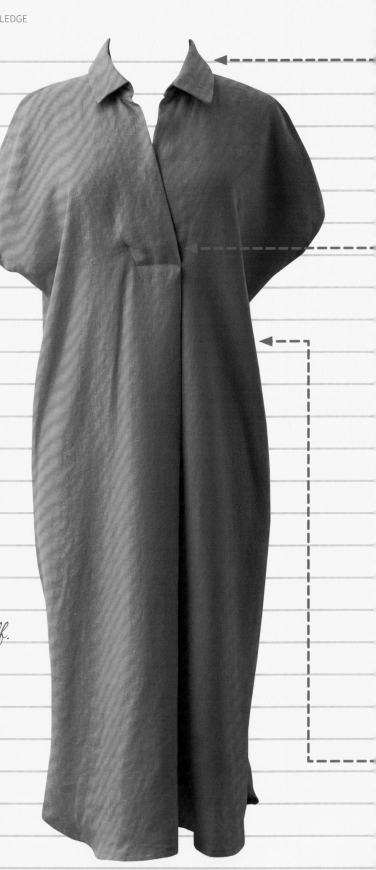

WHICH FABRIC WILL WORK FOR YOUR GARMENT?

How to Feel for Fabric

If you are making something structured—think a blazer-type jacket, a pencil skirt, a dress with pleats, or a coat with top stitching and defining seams—you need a fabric that can hold those lines even during the action of wear. To find out if a particular fabric can do this, lay a good piece over the palm of your hand. A fabric with enough body to succeed in a structured garment won't fall right off the sides of your hand. Look for bend, not flow.

Conversely, fabric with flow is needed for garments that gather and drape, with few seams and details. Rehearse the fabric in your hands—pinch it into gathers or let if fall in folds. Now is your chance to find out how a fabric responds before you commit it to a pattern.

Also consider fabric substance. A single layer in your hands should make you think to yourself, *This is a substantial fabric.*

If you have figure areas, such as a belly shape that would do better with skim than cling, fabrics with body can be kind to yours.

Collar on a stand

Tab-front placket opening into a front pleat

Angled pleat at the back

Don't Be Afraid of Knits

Knit fabrics are a sewing minimalist's dream. Use a good-knits-only pattern, use a ballpoint needle, press minimally, and use a tiny zigzag or even a serger for seaming. I even think knit fabrics are perfect for *beginning* sewists.

Here's why:

⊗ Knit fabrics stretch. Knit garments are easy to wear. Pull on clothing, just down over the head or up over the hips. No need for open-and-close details, such as zippers, buttons, and buttonholes. That's a lot of sewing time saved.

⊗ There is no need for seam finishing. Knits don't fray.

⊗ Knits require only light pressing in specific areas and only after the garment is done.

⊗ Knit patterns typically have fewer pattern pieces. Compare the assembly parts of T-shirt to those of a woven shirt. Most knit garments can be made in an evening after supper.

Choosing knit fabrics is not difficult either, as long as you pay attention to the degree-of-stretch requirements for the pattern.

The most important stretch direction in a knit is crosswise, because the degree of maximum stretch must always run around, not up and down, the body.

So you need to assess the extent of that stretch. These can be expressed in percentages—25% crosswise stretch, for example. Some patterns include a stretch graphic to use to test this cross stretch, or you can refer to this one.

Original piece

20″
17½″
15″
12½″
10″

25%
50%
75%
100%

Knit or Woven? It All Starts with the Fiber

I wouldn't say I am a purist, but I definitely do prefer working with natural fiber fabrics. Fabrics from natural sources are simply easier to sew and more comfortable to wear. However, since they are produced slowly by nature, not quickly by humans, natural fiber fabrics can be more expensive.

Silk matka

Moisture-wicking activewear knit

Wool gabardine

Ponte double-knit

Rayon single knit

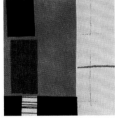

Rayon challis

NATURAL FIBERS

Natural fiber fabrics include those made from cotton, wool, linen, silk, bamboo, hemp, and surprisingly rayon. Rayon is a manufactured fabric, but it is made from wood cellulose. There are many variations of wood cellulose fibers with specific trade names and production method differences, including viscose, Tencel, and modal, but basically they all started with trees, which makes them natural. Also note that many fabrics—cottons and bamboos, for example—are now available too from organic sources.

Apart from origin, structure is another key difference between natural and human-made fibers. The naturals are made up of tiny fragments spun together. Synthetics, in various ways, are extruded into long continuous threads.

A Sewist's View of Natural Fabrics

From our perspective as sewists, natural fabrics have these characteristics:

⊗ They breathe. This is huge. Anyone who has ever spent a night on polyester rather than cotton sheets knows exactly what this means. I always make sure to line my garments with a natural fiber, such as Bemberg rayon, instead of the more usual polyester lining.

⊗ They are easier to stitch. The little spaces between the fiber cells lets a needle slip in and out very easily. This is the reason sewing machine dealers often use substantial cottons as demo fabric—the machine stitches easily and the stitches look great.

⊗ They are absorbent and take dye well. For some fabrics, it can also mean that bright colors, such as red, might also leach out. Hence, old-school instructions to soak these colored fabrics in salt water and/or vinegar make them more colorfast.

⊗ They absorb moisture. Wool can hold up to 30% or even 50% its weight in moisture, which is why Australian and British grandmothers use wool to knit "baby soakers" to be worn over diapers.

⊗ They press well. Natural fibers absorb heat and steam easily and bend with a press. A tighter, harder-finished fabric does this even better than loose weaves. A wool gabardine can hold a crease almost permanently, but a wool flannel may need regular touch-ups with an iron.

⊗ They may not wear as well as synthetics. Some natural fabrics are really strong, such as silk and linen, but the noncontinuous nature of the fibers can cause them to break down more easily on wear areas. Think of how the knees of jeans can thin or how the cuffs of a shirt can fray.

A Sewist's View of Synthetic Fabrics

From a sewist's perspective synthetic fabrics have these characteristics:

- They are generally less expensive in the same way acrylic knitting yarn is far more affordable than wool.

- They will produce clothing that will stand up to hard use. This is why uniforms are often polyester.

- They can pill at wear areas or if subjected to high heat in a dryer. A chemist once told me those little balls in some poly knits were the result of the fibers "frying" when dried. Interesting to think about that one.

- They do not press as well under a home iron but can be creased permanently by commercial pleaters.

- They do not wrinkle easily. Slinky knit is now sometimes described as "travel knit" for this reason.

- They generally don't breathe or absorb body moisture well, although moisture-wicking activewear fabrics are changing this.

- They take surface prints easily. Interlock twist yarn (ITY) can be beautiful in printed knits.

- They can pick up static and cling, polyester wovens in particular.

- They need to be pressed at a lower heat to avoid scorching or even melting.

- They do not absorb stains easily. If my family is coming for red wine and spaghetti, I hope you have some poly on that table

WHAT ABOUT STRETCH WOVENS?

Stretch wovens are any woven with elasticlike threads added for a stretch factor of 4%–10%. Look at the end of the fabric bolt for notations of small percentages of LYCRA (now by INVISTA), spandex, or elastane to identify a stretch woven. Although they are great for comfort, know these fabrics can keep on stretching over the course of a day. Be prepared for that.

The Mechanics of Fabric Construction

Just as interesting as fiber sources, and as important to your matching of fabric to garment or pattern, is the way fabrics themselves are constructed. Essentially, there are two categories: woven and knits. Within each category, there are some really interesting, even historic, variations.

WOVEN FABRICS

Many plain old classic fabrics, such as cotton, linen, silk, and wool, are often woven with the basic over-and-under technique. These fabrics are called *plain weaves*. There is not a right or a wrong side in these fabrics, which is helpful to know when you are cutting. Of course, many fabrics are not plain weaves. The combos are interesting.

Here are some of those weave variations.

Twills are fabrics in which the cross threads jump over two or more lengthwise threads in staggered patterns, creating tiny diagonal ridges and a strong fabric. Denims and gabardine are made this way. Twills most often have a discernable right and wrong side. On the diagonal, they drape fairly well, if not gather. They also bounce back reliably from wrinkles.

Satin-weave fabrics can be made of any fiber, even cotton, which is called *sateen*. All satin weaves have some shine because crosswise threads "float" over a number of the vertical threads and are thus able to catch the light. Be aware, however, that the floats are vulnerable to picking and snags. Definitely smooth your rough gardening hands before you work with satins.

Nap weaves are easy to identify. Corduroy, velvet, velveteen, and terry are all wovens with one napped surface. The nap of all these fabrics, particularly of corduroy and velvet, has a definite direction, like the fur on a cat or dog. Each direction has a specific shade, too. A pile that runs up the body will always be a richer color than one that runs down. As a result, you must lay out all pattern pieces in the same direction so that the color is consistent throughout the garment. Look for the "with nap" yardage requirements and layout advice.

Remember as well that these fabrics show pin and needle marks, so they need to be pinned and basted within the seam allowance. Walking or even-feed feet, integrated or attached as a special foot, will make these fabrics less likely to slip while stitching. It's also a good idea when sewing pile fabrics to use a tiny zigzag rather than a straight stitch for seaming. The zigzag lets some of the pile free and creates a less obvious seamline.

KNIT FABRICS

You won't be surprised to know that knit fabrics are knitted, not woven. The behavior and character of different knit fabrics is determined by how they are made and the fiber they are made from. Linen and cotton knits, for example, tend to have less bounce and stretch than those made of inherently stretchy fibers, such as wool. If you are a knitter, the most common types of knitted fabric will be familiar to you.

Single knits, often labeled as jersey, have a very clear right and wrong side—think of the knit versus purl sides of stockinette-stitch knitting. Single knits curl to the right side and don't have quite the bounce-back (recovery) of double- or rib knits. Garments with draping or cowl necks as well as undergarments frequently call for single knits/jerseys. These fabrics are often knit on giant circular looms, and then the tubes are cut open to make flat yardage. These cut edges frequently are sealed with glue dots you might notice.

Ribbing knits are distinctive and easily recognizable. They are made of different combinations of alternating knit and purl stitches and look pretty much the same on both sides. Ribbings are used mainly in closures around necklines and wrists and along the bottom of garments, much like ribbings are used in hand knitting.

Interlocks are actually very fine rib fabrics, with two smooth, identical sides and have more weight than single knits. If single knits are used for T-shirt type tops, interlocks are the knit fabric of choice for dresses and more structured pants and tops.

Double-knits are made with two interlocking fibers, much like double hand knitting. Double-knit is thick, stable, recovers well (bounces back when stretched), and has the body for structured and almost tailored knit garments. It does not usually have a right or wrong side. Ponte and scuba knit are double-knit fabrics.

Mysterious Names for Fabrics

Many pattern envelopes specify fabrics that don't match any labels at the fabric store. This is not helpful to shopping sewists.

So here are my translations of some of the less familiar fabric designations:

Bengaline traditionally was a tightly woven fabric with a definite strong crosswise thread. More recently it often refers to a stretch woven fabric, usually in various combinations of polyester, rayon, or nylon and viscose (a kind of rayon), and an elastic fiber such as spandex. Bengaline stretch wovens, unlike other stretch wovens and knits for that matter, are stretchy along the *length*—not along the width, like knits—so must be laid out with the "straight-of-grain" lines running perpendicular to the selvage edge. As with other forms of stretch fabric, woven or knit, it is important to maintain the greatest stretch around the body.

Challis is another descriptor for a soft flowing fabric. Often associated with rayon or wool, typically challis is surface printed, usually with something floral or a paisley.

China silk is a plain-weave thin silk. If you order this online for garments, be aware that many china silks are used only for lining and might be too lightweight for garment construction.

Crepe de chine doesn't need much translation—you don't need a degree in romance fabrics to figure out that this one refers to a kind of silk crepe. Any lightweight fabric with a drapey hand can be used in a pattern that calls for crepe de chine.

Cloque is a term sometimes seen on the backs of pattern envelopes for structured knit tops or dresses. The term cloque can refer to either a knit or woven fabric with a distinctive pebbly appearance. When this is a fabric requirement, use a fabric with body and some bounce, often a double-knit.

Dupioni is an iconic dressy fabric. If it weren't for silk dupioni, the mothers-of-the-grooms in this world would all be naked. Silk dupioni is a plain weave, crisp, heavy silk with definite uneven weight threads, often iridescent, making it more exotic than similar taffeta. I was once told that the silk filament used to weave dupioni is actually doubled, created when two cocoons grow together, which come to think of it makes the fabric particularly suitable for wedding wear. Dupioni is easy to sew and presses well. However, it is not suited to a lot of easing in, which can make princess seams and close set-in sleeves a challenge. A similar lighter version of this fabric is *shantung*, which unlike dupioni is often now woven from synthetic fibers.

Faille (sometimes described as *tissue faille*) is a term is rarely seen on fabric bolts, so I am not sure why patterns still refer to it. A faille is a kind of lightweight woven rib with a soft flowing hand. Any soft flowy fabric of any fiber would work here.

Flannel and flannelette are synonyms for cozy. I have a soft spot for flannelette Christmas nightgowns always made of this plain-weave cotton fabric with only one fuzzy side. Flannel is fuzzy on both sides and can be made from cotton, wool, or blends in a plain or twill weave.

Gabardine is sometimes also referred to as *gab*. This fabric is a classic—a fine, closely woven twill. Gabardine can be made of wool, blends, or synthetics, if for uniforms. Good wool gab presses well with steam and pressing tools, such as a tailor's clapper. It takes topstitching very well. Because of its close weave and smooth, tight finish, some classic all-weather coats are made with gabardine.

Georgette can be thought of as a heavier version of chiffon with a slightly textured surface. Georgettes can be made of synthetics, which are slippery, or silk, which has a drier hand that sticks to itself a bit, a real help at the machine. This fabric definitely calls for the smallest machine needle (sharps #60), thin silk or cotton thread, and more nerves than I have to sew.

Guipure is a heavy lace distinguished by the heavy cord around and as connection between the motifs. It is called for in fitted lace bodices or lace sheath dresses to preserve the lines that would be lost if made in a lighter-weight, mesh-based lace.

Lawn is an old-school fabric that appears to be making a comeback after a long retirement, encouraged I think by the desire to make simple woven tops but without the bulk of quilting cottons. Lawns are thin fabrics, tightly woven with a smooth silky finish that resists wrinkles. Liberty of London made cotton lawns famous.

Microfiber can be thought of the synthetic world's response to silk and in some ways takes that even further. In the natural world, silk is the thinnest fiber with an individual strand of one denier. A microfiber is any human-made fabric with filaments finer than even this. The actual type of synthetic fiber (polyester or nylon, for example) can vary, as can the mechanical production, knitted or woven. Many suede-like fabrics are microfibers, known for durability and stain resistance. Microfibers can be tricky to sew due to the typically high thread count. To counter this, use a special microtex needle and try to avoid styles with too many seams and construction details.

Muslin is a fabric that has also become the name of a garment, as when a sewist talks about "making a muslin." In this case the muslin is understood to be a fitting garment made out a stable, plain-woven, unbleached cotton fabric. Muslin is widely available and sometimes comes in superwide widths, which can be handy when rehearsing patterns or fine-tuning the fit.

Peau de soie brings back memories. It seems to me that my mother and grandmother talked a lot about peau de soie. I associate peau de soie with a heavy satin with a matte sheen, originally made of silk but these days more often made of synthetics and therefore appropriately disguised with a French name.

Percale sounds like a bed sheet, but it is really a plain-weave, high-thread-count cotton fabric distinguished by the same number of threads per inch up and down, ensuring consistent strength. (Fabrics are interesting aren't they?)

Pique is a textured fabric with a dominant lengthwise rib in either a cotton or blend. I am partial to cotton pique shift dresses as they have both the comfort and breathability of all cottons but enough structure to hold the most retro A-line shape.

Silk noil is actually silk but doesn't look it. This fabric is characterized by a fairly rough surface and is made of the waste materials left over from finer silks. With a dry and pleasant hand, silk noil is easy to sew—needles pierce it well—and has warmth and breathability. Although it drapes and takes dye easily, silk noil can sag over time as the fibers do not have a continuous structure. For this reason I would save the silk noil for loose, unstructured styles such as unlined kimono jackets.

Organza and organdy are much like flannelette and flannel—these two terms seem interchangeable but they are not. *Organdy* is made of cotton and is thin, with a crisp hand, and often with a finish applied to make it stiffer. Good-quality organdies are used as sew-in interfacing, and this finish is permanent. In less-expensive organdy interfacing, this stiffening may vanish in the wash—one good reason to always pretreat (page 135) all fabrics, even interfacings. *Organza* is the upscale version of organdy and is made from synthetics or silk. Silk organza is a wonderful fabric. It has the combination of glamour (you can spot a real silk organza wedding dress from the back pew) with a wide assortment of great uses in the sewing room as well. I use it as a see-through pressing cloth, to underline loose weaves for stability without body, and as a sew-in interfacing. In case you are interested, silk organza is lint free, so it also makes primo jelly bags for canning.

Ottoman is a kind of rib fabric with the ribs running, very dominantly crosswise. Traditionally this was a woven fabric often used in evening coats and purses (you see it a lot in vintage clothing from the 1950s), but ottoman knits are more ordinary now. Any double-knit can be used when ottoman is called for.

Seersucker is another of my all-time favorite fabrics. Made of cotton or cotton blends, the distinctive rippled stripes of seersuckers lift the fabric away from the body to allow airflow. Popular for summer suits and shirts for men, no other fabric is cooler, in my opinion, with only linen a close second. I have used seersucker to make crib sheets for summer babies and for nightgowns—without which I would not have survived menopause.

Stable knit is to me a contradiction in terms—I am always a bit wary when I read "woven or stable knit." I would feel the same way about a recipe that told me to cook something in either a microwave or oven for 30 minutes. Patterns that call for stable knits, in my experience, tend to produce knit garments with too much ease. Use a knits-only pattern for knits, even the stable ones, and stick to wovens for any pattern that says "woven fabrics or stable knits."

Tulle should make you think bridal veil. Tulle is much softer than regular netting, can be gathered to make comfortable sleeve heads in puffed formal sleeves, and used as an underlining to add some body with little bulk. A full skirt underlined in tulle will really stand away from the body with great prom dress puffiness.

Viyella is a fabric I am including in the list in case you run across some somewhere and know to buy it and send it to me. I will pay you back. Viyella is a 50/50 wool and cotton fine twill shirting fabric that dads used to wear, and like dads, improves with age.

THE BACKUP FABRICS: INTERFACING AND LININGS

Interfacing

You need a good interfacing, and you need the right one, to make great clothes. Unfortunately there are too many choices. Fortunately, the guidelines are few and you only need a few standbys to get through.

INTERFACING SHOULD ACT AND MOVE LIKE THE FABRIC

A woven fabric needs a woven interfacing; a knit needs a knit.

Nothing needs one of those paper, fiber types that are neither woven nor knit. Avoid those. Incidentally only two interfacings have been used for the garments in this book: a tricot fusible stretch knit for the knit fabrics and fusible woven for the woven fabrics.

SOME SITUATIONS CALL FOR SEW-INS

Sew-ins are a great choice when a soft hand or a roll is needed—in a shawl collar, for example. They are also the interfacings of choice in thin and fine fabrics, such as lawns, in which fusing might show through. In either case, do not let the interfacing extend into the seam allowances; this just adds unwanted bulk and makes pressing difficult. When using a sew-in, pin or baste it to each piece before stitching and later trim it away close to the stitching line. Areas where the sew-in interfacing is not caught in a seamline should, of course, be secured with tiny, somewhat loose catch stitches (page 202).

DON'T BE AFRAID OF FUSIBLES

Old-style fusible interfacings were about as subtle as a paper plate stuck to the garment, but those days are long past.

These days a fusible interfacing should work very well in most garment sewing. Just make sure you trim the seam allowances from the interfacing before you apply it, and know how to fuse.

Here's how to fuse successfully:

⊗ Read the manufacturer's instructions first. Some fusibles require steam to set; others require a dry iron.

⊗ Use a pressing cloth, lean into the iron, and press up and down—don't glide the iron.

⊗ Just like you don't ever, ever move the iron around while fusing, don't move the fabric until it is completely cool either. Remember the heat of the iron has temporarily melted the fusing glue. Letting the fabric cool before moving gives the glue a chance to set and will prevent fused-in wrinkles.

⊗ Fuse first from the wrong side and then again from the right side. Heat on the right side helps pull the glue into the fabric.

⊗ Keep in mind, too, that the fusing glue also adds weight. As a result, always use an interfacing with a lighter hand than the fabric so the process doesn't over stiffen the areas of the garment to which interfacing has been applied.

Linings

For some reason, lining no longer has the usual role it once had in sewing. This is a mystery to me. Patterns for garments that should be lined, such as jackets and coats, now come described as easy and unlined, as if that was a virtue.

Linings add so much to clothing.

Here is my list:

⊗ Linings finish the inside and cover all sorts of random construction details—seam allowances and hem edges; the long sides of facings and the wrong sides of pockets, zippers, gathers, pleats, and darts. They cover sleeve heads and shoulder pads. They cover mistakes.

⊗ Linings do the heavy lifting of being a garment. They absorb strain and perspiration. They wrinkle and crease so the outer garment won't have to. Lined clothes look better and last longer than those that are not.

⊗ Linings make a garment easier to wear. Jackets and coats slip on and off shoulders. Arms slide down sleeves. Backs don't ride up and stick when you stand up after sitting down.

⊗ Linings can make a garment warmer. Flannel-backed satins add warmth and the kind of weight that makes a wool coat hang right. Fleece on the inside of a jacket body gives comfort on a cold day. Underline a snow jacket lining with a needle-punch and/or put chamois into the back of a dress coat and you'll be ready for Winnipeg in January.

⚙ Linings mean you don't have to wear a slip. Yes I know a lot of people don't wear slips these days, but many of them should. In addition to preventing show-through in light fabrics, lining stops skirt creep, particularly with tights, which seems to me to be a good thing.

⚙ Linings are interesting. Sometimes I like my lining fabric even more than I like the exterior fabric. Linings can be fun and a bit nutty—the surprise that is a glimpse. A gray jacket with a bright turquoise lining can be terrific. A patterned silk lining in a coat and a blouse to match seems to me to be the height of chic.

So once you accept that linings are important, you can't just settle for any old bargain polyester lining like the ready-to-wear folks use.

Go for quality and breathability. I like silk linings and more economically Bemberg rayon lining.

PRETREATING FABRICS

I preshrink all my fabrics before I cut. It makes sense to do to the fabric what will be done to the eventual garment.

If the garment will be machine washed and dried, or machine washed and line dried, do the same to the yardage as soon as you bring it home. This helps prevent surprises after the first wash.

Cottons and Rayons

For 100% cotton and rayon fabrics of all kinds, I actually pretreat twice to get as much of the shrinkage out of the fabric as I can. Cottons, particularly loosely woven ones or twills, such as denims, can lose as much as a few inches per yard in shrinking, more when you wash it more than once.

Knits

Knits, of course, can be washed. If you line dry, remember that the degree of greatest stretch runs crosswise. If you can, try to hang a knit lengthwise.

Wools

You can preshrink wools by steaming at the ironing board, but doing that with more than 6 yards of 60″ gabardine with a domestic iron is more than I can stand, although stronger women can and should.

My own method for sanely pretreating wool is to run a tricot slip or something that picks up very little water through the rinse/spin cycle of the washing machine then put that damp item in the dryer with the wool. Ten minutes on a low heat will shrink the wool just enough without changing it perceptively.

Linens

Linens can be pretreated the same way as wools and maintained with a lot of ironing and spray starch. To avoid the work of this upkeep, some folks wash and machine dry their linen yardage before they cut. Of course, this drastically changes the hand of the linen from crisp to soft and may also fade the color a bit; but once done, a linen garment can then be washed and worn as is without much ironing thereafter. The pink linen dress featured in this chapter was made from washed linen, because I see this as an everyday dress.

Silks

Some silks can also be hand prewashed. If you do this, just make sure to iron the damp fabric dry to get the wrinkles out, and use a pressing cloth. Personally, I wash all but the heavy, fancy silks because it heads off the water spot issue, which can turn something as innocent as baby drool into a permanent stain. It's so much easier to turn the fabric into one giant water spot right from the start so any incidental drops of water that come after won't show.

ONTO THE TABLE: LAYOUT TIPS

After your fabric has been pretreated, it is ready to put on the cutting table and lay out the pattern.

The key when working with woven fabrics is, of course, to make sure that all pieces are laid on grain. This is easy to do by measuring from each end of the grain arrow printed on pattern pieces to the selvage (finished, not cut) edge. In folded fabric take care to match the selvage edges, not the cut edges that are so often a little crooked.

Laying out knit fabrics can be a bit trickier, primarily because some knits can curl and don't lie as flat on the table. Letting the knit fabric rest for a few hours before cutting can help, but if the fabric seems particularly resistant to smoothing, the solution is to cut out pieces single layer.

Learning to cut out pattern pieces from a single layer of fabric is a useful skill. In addition to helping cut some knits, single-layer cutting is so helpful when working with a fabric with a definite print design or stripe you want to match.

Because it takes a bit of skill, matching stripes or print motifs in details is a mark of a quality garment and a savvy sewist. Being that savvy sewist is easy.

Note that when purchasing fabric, extra is always needed to match prints or stripes.

And last, but not least … if you fall in love with a fabric that has motifs printed in various directions, take your time to study how the motifs will look on your finished garment. In the sleeveless top (at right), I loved the figures on the fabric, especially the Audrey Hepburn–like model in the black dress, which is near the upper arms on the finished top. So I placed her right side up and let the others fall in any direction. When the top was finished, most of the figures at center front were upside down. Lesson learned, again.

MINI LESSON

Cutting Striped Fabric Single Layer

Since you work one pattern piece at a time when cutting single layer, it makes sense to start with a main pattern piece cut on the fold:

1. Working single layer, pin and carefully cut out the front pattern piece, stopping the cut right at the fold line.

2. Remove the pattern piece from the fabric and flip the cut section over at the fold line, right sides together.

3. Carefully arrange the cut piece so its stripes line up perfectly with the layer of fabric underneath. Complete cutting out the front following the cut edges of the first front half.

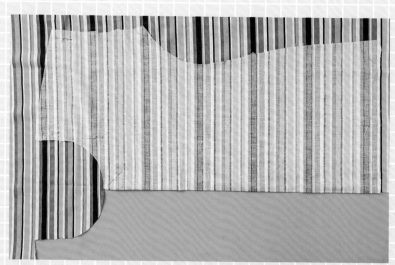

For every subsequent pattern piece, such as the back or sleeves, lay the previously cut piece on top of the single layer of uncut fabric to help line up the next pattern piece. At right, the cut front is laid on the fabric, stripe matching stripe, to help position the sleeve pattern on the fabric to match the front piece to which it will attach.

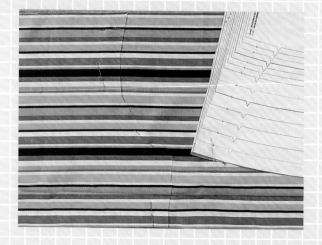

MINI LESSON

How to Match Print Motifs

When I figured out this easy print-matching technique for pockets, I just felt clever. I hope this method makes you feel the same way. Here's how to do it:

1. Mark the pocket placement on the shirt front with 2 tailor tacks stitched into the large dots that are always marked on the pattern piece for this purpose (page 198).

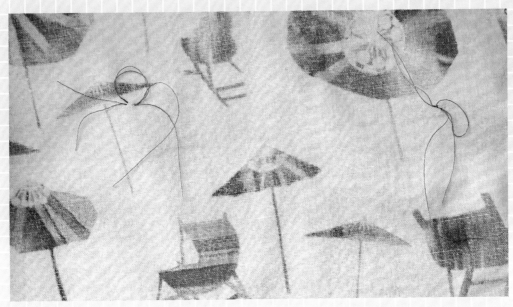

2. Place a largish scrap of fabric over the shirt front and arrange it so the various print motifs are directly over each other. When you are satisfied with the match, pin the scrap fabric in place on the garment front.

3. Working from the wrong side of the shirt, put a pin through the tailor tack markings right through the both layers (garment and scrap fabric) of the shirt front, so you can see the pins on the right side of the fabric scrap pinned to the shirt front.

4. Pin the pocket paper pattern piece to the fabric scrap using the pins you placed in Step 3 to help you place the pattern piece accurately.

5. Carefully unpin and lift off the fabric scrap, with the pattern pinned to it, from the shirt front and cut out the pocket piece.

6. Fold and sew the pocket hem. Press under the seam allowances on the remaining sides of the pocket. Repin the pocket piece to the shirt front (the prints should match exactly) and stitch the pocket in place.

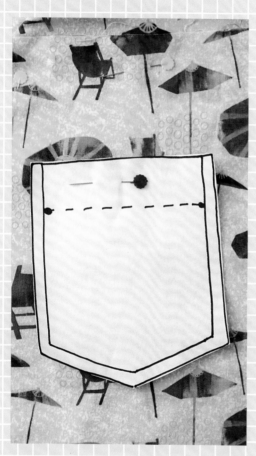

Who's to know how easy this is!

Barbara's Tips

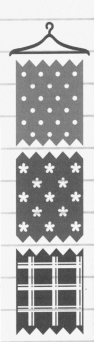

✓ Washing Silk

When hand washing silk, either before you sew with it or after the garment is made, add some white vinegar to the rinse water. This will remove any trace of soap and help the fabric retain the dye and stay bright longer.

✓ Cutting Slippery Fabrics

It can be hard to cut slippery fabrics. Pins can shift as you cut, making it hard to cut accurately. I find using weights, beach rocks, or the old standby—tuna fish cans—very helpful here. The trick is to place the weights at key points and to lay your flat palm next to the scissors, cut a scissor length, and then reposition your hand for the next cut. If your fabric still seems to slide away under your scissors, try laying paper under the fabric and cut through both as you go. I often do this when I work with difficult-to-cut fabrics using wax paper from the kitchen drawer.

✓ Finding the Maximum Stretch

Not sure how to find the direction of maximum stretch in two-way knit? Pull on it. The direction of greatest stretch, which needs to go around the body, has more bounce back; the direction of less stretch, less.

✓ The Magic of Bias

The maximum stretch in knits generally runs perpendicular to the selvage edge and across the width. In a woven fabric, the degree of greatest stretch is along the bias. Any woven fabric will behave knitlike and most stretchy when cut along the bias. The wonderful aspect of bias: Bindings cut on the bias stretch will not ravel, making them perfect for necklines, bias-cut trims, and treatments such as Hong Kong finishes (page 242). No real need to finish the seam allowances on bias-cut fabrics.

✓ Finding Coordinating Colors

Printed yardage and home decorator fabrics in particular have small boxes of every color used in the print along the selvage. These marks are useful reference points when choosing coordinating fabrics.

✓ Estimating Yardage on the Bolt

Unsure if the bolt has enough fabric for you? Count the folds at the end of the bolt on one side of the cardboard core—two folds represent roughly one yard of fabric.

✓ Testing Fabrics

If you can't decide whether a fabric is natural or synthetic, do the burn test. Take a small piece, stand over the bathroom sink, and set it on fire. If the flame produces ash, the fabric is a natural fiber. If it curls quickly into a ball without any ash, the fiber is human-made.

✓ Mesh Linings

Mesh fashion knits make great all-purpose lining for any knit garment and will hang without static.

✓ Choosing Fabric for Kids

Children judge clothing as much by feel—cozy or cold, for example—as color and design, so keep this in mind when selecting fabric for a young person.

7 *The Gear* Side of Sewing

THERE ARE THREE THINGS THAT IMPROVE A NEW OR RETURNING SEWIST'S EXPERIENCE: a place where you can leave your equipment up and ready to go (It's amazing how much you can get done while you burn dinner!), a decent machine, and a few of the right tools.

Microsuede never wrinkles.

Elastic waistband faced with cotton print

Perfect for traveling

A PLACE TO SEW

I am not one of those ideal sewing room people. I am not a fan of those beautiful floor plans that show U-shaped setups where a productive sewist can sew, press, and serge without ever standing up. Get up and walk around. It's good for you.

I have my machines in my basement and an ironing board on my main floor. Absorbed in a project, I can clock 10,000 steps easily on the stairs up and down between pressing and stitching. My kind of workout.

I like to think sewing stations as opposed to a sewing room, although you can have both. Here are some ideas for that.

A Sewing Station

A sewing station is where your machine lives, ready to go for drive-by sewing.

Have basic machine gear handy, too. I keep a cutlery drawer organizer filled with my bobbins, needles, best machine feet, and seam ripper behind my machine. I also have a big squishy pincushion to the right of the machine for pins I take out while I sew, and to the left there's a kid's cereal bowl for loose thread ends.

That's it. The only other essential is ample good task lighting; something gooseneck that you can aim at the working area is great. My new fancy BERNINA has great, bright runway lighting I appreciate, but my older and much loved machines do not. Get good lighting any way that you can set up.

Some folks also have a bulletin board to stick up the instructions, if you are the kind of sewist who follows those (my friend Sue never did and used to call them the destructions). If a bulletin board is not practical, put a piece of clear vinyl under your machine to hold the words you need to read.

Double-cut front, each layer hemmed separately

Lettuce trim (page 174)

A Pressing Station

A pressing station is a place you can leave an ironing board up. In the house I once lived in, there was an ironing board that dropped down from a cupboard in the kitchen—how practical is that? But I haven't seen one in a house since.

So find somewhere to set up an ironing board and remember it's a working surface too. You have to be able to lean into it to get a good press in many fabrics. The old heavy yard-sale ones are best; avoid those rickety numbers the stores now sell. Stay clear of those shiny silver ironing board covers, too. They reflect too much heat and you might end up frying your fabric on it, particularly synthetics. Pad your ironing board with a good old 100% wool blanket (wool holds and returns heat and steam nicely) and cover it with a cotton cloth.

Look for the heaviest iron you can find and afford. Fill it with the type of water the manufacturer specifies and empty the iron between uses; this avoids the awful surprise of rust spraying out onto your best project.

And whatever you do, avoid those automatic shut-off irons—nothing is more annoying when pressing as you sew. If you find it hard to get a good iron without a shut-off these days, look for more professional versions, available online and from fabric retailers. Old-school heavy, turn-them-on-and-they-will-stay-on irons are often available at yard sales, too; just make sure the cords are still in good shape. If you have a leave-on iron but are still worried about burning the house down, plug your iron and a light into a power strip and turn it off when you leave the room.

Under your ironing board, put a basket for a seam roll, ham, clapper, and pressing cloths.

Remember that all good pressing tools are made of wood or packed hardwood sawdust. Wood fiber, even in a hard roll of industrial paper towel, the kind you see in public restrooms, captures heat and steam and sends it back into the fabric to extend the value of the press. A good seam roll is your most important pressing tool. The rounded surface of the roll will let you press along the stitching line *only* and avoid having the pressed-in seam allowance show through.

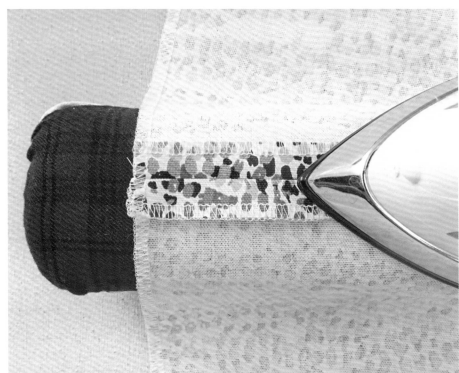

A tailor's ham is also an essential; you simply can't get a nice press on a curved edge by flattening it onto the ironing board. A ham like this has many curves, so you can always find one to match your dart, hip, or princess seam.

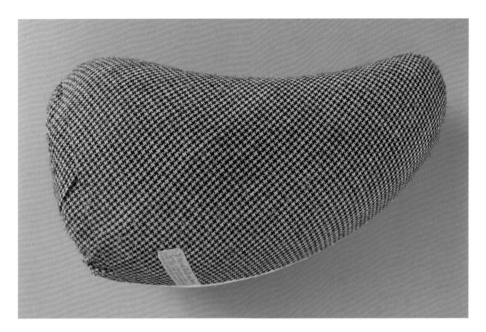

Tailor's hams are also enormously useful when making collars, particularly those with wool or fabric with some memory to them. To use a ham to put a roll line into a collar, set up your ham vertically. You can use a ham holder, some cans, or the vice on the workbench in the garage. Next, wrap your collar around it like a neck. Shoot this unit full of steam and let it dry. Presto, a beautifully shaped, already-pressed collar ready for insertion into the garment.

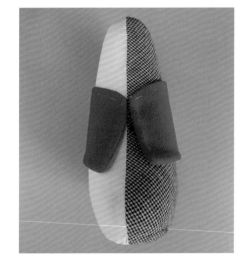

Make sure there is a tailor's clapper in your toolkit, too. Basically a hard wood block, this tool is pressed down hard on an edge after a good burst of steam, producing a really sharp crease—think gabardine edges or denim hems. Clappers are often combined with point presses—miniature Barbie doll–size ironing boards mounted on top—useful for pressing open little seams on collars and cuffs.

Clapper point presser

Pressing open a collar

A Hand-Sewing Station

I also think a portable hand-sewing station is important. In most sewing projects, there is some hand work to be done—buttons to be sewn on, hems to be stitched, facings to be tacked. To my mind, these are tired sewist's jobs and to be done with your feet up watching Netflix.

A little sewing basket with hand-sewing needles, small scissors, a few pins, and some threads is very useful.

A Place to Cut

You will note that I have not included a cutting station in all of this because most folks don't have room. Right now, I have a nice big cutting table the husband put up on risers because I am tall. But over my lifetime I have done most of my cutting out on dining room tables. I also own one of those cardboard foldout cutting mats that I take with me when I travel (okay, I don't pack light). I can put that over a bed, on a picnic table, on top of a kitchen island, and once over a stove (turned off) to cut.

THE BIG GEAR: SEWING MACHINES AND ACCESSORIES

The most important relationship in your sewing life is the one between you and your sewing machine. As in all relationships, communication is key. You have to do your part. Make sure you understand why a machine does what it does.

I used to know a service technician who would often tell me "the problem is in the chair" when I complained about a machine. Often his "repair" work turned into user education. I would like to pass some of that on to you. Let's start with some of the most common sewing machine frustrations and talk about why they might be happening.

Possible Frustrations of the Person in the Chair

FRUSTRATION 1: FABRIC JAMS

Fabric goes down the rabbit hole in the throat plate at the beginning of a seam and gets stuck there.

Why this happens: Zigzag sewing machines have a wide hole in the throat plate so the needle has room to swing sideways. At the beginning of a seam, before the fabric has fully covered this hole, the needle can inadvertently push fine fabrics down into the bobbin area and cause a jam.

Solution: There are several things you can do so this doesn't happen. The first and a more immediate fix is to move the cut edge back a bit at the beginning of the seam, so the cut edge isn't hanging over the opening for that first stitch. Second, try moving the needle position over to the side of the opening; this will reduce the area of the opening in the throat plate. Or you could change to a single-needle hole throat plate (some brands also have a single-hole straight-stitch foot) to reduce the opening even further. Here (at right) is

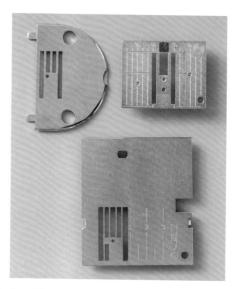

what a straight-stitch plate looks like, which should make clear why these little devices are so useful.

Third, and this is works well with stretchy knits, start the seam with a scrap butted up behind the cut edge, creating an on-ramp or leader into the seam, which can be cut away when you are done.

FRUSTRATION 2: INITIAL THREAD TANGLES

You notice a ball of messy thread in the first few stitches of the stitching.

Why this happens: When you start to sew, the thread tail from the bobbin gets caught in the first few stitches.

Solution: If you remember to hold both thread tails at the beginning of a seam out and back to the left so they don't tangle, you can make this problem go away. Using a scrap leader as noted previously will also work.

FRUSTRATION 3: RANDOM SHORT STITCHES

You turn a corner when topstitching, say around a collar, and the stitches suddenly get shorter.

Why this happens: These short stitches are caused because the presser foot has lost level contact with the throat plate and consequently lost its ability to feed the fabric consistently. Looking at a side view of the foot, you would see the toe move up, and the back of the foot down and off the fabric, as the corner is turned.

Solution: As you approach the corner of a collar, stop stitching with the needle down, lift the presser foot, and add a little shim under the back of the foot to keep it level. I use a fabric compensator tool to do this. Other sewists use layers of fabric or cardboard for the same purpose. Once the foot moves off the leveling helper, remove it.

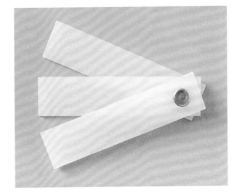

FRUSTRATION 4: FABRIC SHIFTING

You start sewing with two identical lengths of fabric, but by the end of the seam, one layer seems to have grown longer.

Why this happens: This is a fairly common issue since the tiny teeth of the feed dogs tend to pick up the bottom layer of the fabric slightly while the presser foot tends to push the top layer forward a bit. This can be more apparent in thin or stretchy fabrics.

Solution: Counteract this process by installing a walking foot attachment or by using a built-in even-feed foot—both of which have top feed dogs to balance the action of those under the presser foot. You really will be able to feel the extra control with your hands on the fabric. Walking feet of any kind are also so useful when tricky lining up is necessary—when sewing stripes or plaids, for example—or when sewing slippery surface fabrics like sheers, velvets, or leather.

FRUSTRATION 5: BOBBIN "BIRD'S NEST"

The right side of the stitch looks great but the underside is a mess, a real "bird's nest."

Why this happens: First don't worry that this is an issue with your lower tension. What's happened here is the upper thread has slipped out of or missed some control spot in the upper threading, likely the tension disks. As a result, it has just gathered down in the bobbin case. Just like a rope thrown out of a window, I used to explain to my sewing students—you just end up with a messy pile down below.

Solution: Rethread the top of the machine carefully. Make sure when threading the top of the machine to always do this with the foot up. A raised presser foot opens the tension disks so the thread can fit in there snuggly.

FRUSTRATION 6: RANDOM LONG STITCHES

Random long stitches appear out of nowhere when sewing knits or some synthetics.

Why this happens: These long stitches are called "skipped stitches." Consider them evidence that the needle has unsuccessfully and repeatedly tried to get through the fabric, but it can't puncture and has just bounced along the surface of the fabric until it can get though.

Solution: To eliminate skipped stitches, switch up to a ballpoint needle for knits, which will spread rather than try to pierce the fabrics and will therefore let the needle complete the stitch. With really thick synthetic knits, such as a scuba knit, I sometimes also stitch through a fabric softener sheet to coat the needle before I start sewing.

Needles: The Whole Point of the Machine

Skipped stitches are a good reminder that the tiny surface of a sewing machine needle does all the real work of stitch formation. Using the right needle can make all the difference. Here are some guidelines to help you choose that right needle.

USE THE SMALLEST NEEDLE YOU CAN

Most of us think multiple layers or thick fabric automatically call for a large machine needle. Not necessarily so. An analogy helps. Think of hanging a picture on a wall. What goes easier into a wall? A small, sharp nail or a big old wood dowel? Same works for fabric. Fine and sharp makes the best stitch. I use a denim #70 needle for general natural fiber sewing and a microtex #70 for synthetic wovens. For a very fine fabric, such as a silk georgette, I use a #60 and a shorter stitch length to get a nice pucker-free stitch.

DON'T USE UNIVERSAL NEEDLES IF YOU CAN HELP IT

I have to confess; I don't use universal needles at all. They remind me of my dad, who used to serve rosé wine so both the red wine and the white wine drinkers were happy. Didn't really work with either group. Use sharps for wovens. Use ballpoints, sometimes labeled jersey or "for knits" needles, for knits.

CONSIDER SPECIALTY NEEDLES

Each specialty needle in its own way will solve a stitching issue for you. Here are some of my favorites:

Leather needles   The wedge shape of a leather needle keeps the leather from grabbing the needle and not letting go as the stitch is formed, therefore forming skipped stitches. I also reach for a leather needle in those when-all-else-has-failed situations, mending a tent, for example.

Topstitch needles   I have to put in an endorsement for these. Wow, how come more people don't know about topstitch needles? The long, large eye of these needles takes thicker threads easily and avoids those top-stitching jams.

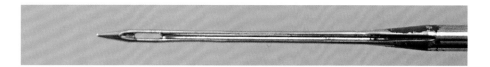

Twin-needles   These needles come in varying widths and sharp and ballpoint varieties. They are easily recognizable by the two machine needles mounted in a single shaft. Twins can be used in any sewing machine that does a straight stitch as long as that machine has a top- or front-loading bobbin case, but not one that loads on the side as in a vintage Singer Featherweight, for example.

Twin needles also put two threads in the upper thread path (that's why you may have a spare spindle on the machine or in your accessory kit), one for each needle. The two threads force the bobbin thread to move back and forth, creating a stretchy sort of zigzag stitch on the underside of the fabric.

Because of this bobbin action, any twin-needle stitch, like all zigzags, is by definition stretchy, which makes it perfect for knit hems and top stitching. When using a twin needle, stitch at a slow steady pace. If you experience "tunneling" between the stitching, try using either a closer-set twin needle, stitching with a stabilizer under the fabric (one of my students used cheap toilet paper), interfacing the hem with a fusible tricot interfacing, or using wooly nylon in the bobbin. Here are some twin-needles. Note that they come in a wide variety of widths with both sharp for woven and ballpoint for knits points.

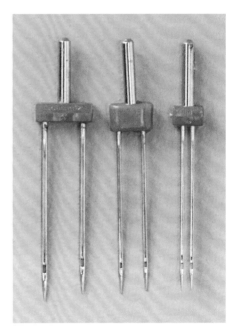

And below is a twin-needle hem. From the top of the fabric you would see 2 parallel rows of top stitching. From the back, you would see the bobbin thread zigzag between both lines of thread.

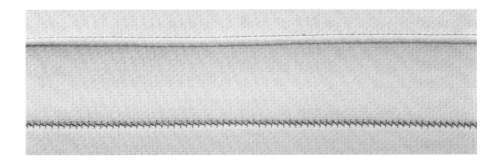

How to Maximize Any Machine

In machines, as in life, it is really important to make the most of what you have.

With sewing machines, this means exploring accessories. In addition to a walking foot or an even-feed foot, here are my favorites and what they do for my sewing.

A SATIN STITCH OR APPLIQUÉ FOOT

You might own an appliqué foot and not know it. Turn over your all-purpose presser feet. You will probably find that one of these has a cutout ridge on the bottom. This is your appliqué foot. That cutout lets tightly packed satin stitches flow through without sticking. Often these feet have an open toe for better visibility when doing decorative stitching.

A QUILTING BAR

This is another wonderful standard attachment found in most accessory kits. A quilting bar is basically a rod that is screwed into the needle bar above the foot. It is used to help measure regular distances between lines of stitching and is perfect when working with a larger fabric area that covers the seam markings on the throat plate.

AN EDGE-STITCHING FOOT

This foot has a ledge to the side that, in combination with needle positions, helps to top-stitch or ditch stitch without wobbles. Really, unless you are one of those really rare sewists who was born with a straight eye, you really would enjoy an edge-stitch foot.

A FLAT FELLING OR LAP FOOT

This is one of my favorite feet because it is such a time-saver. This foot is essential for jeans and shirts and makes perfect flat-felled seams so easily.

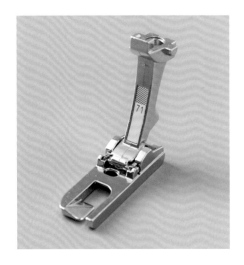

MINI LESSON

Making a Flat-Felled Seam

1. Trim the regular ⅝″ seam allowance of the fabric layer that will be under the top-stitched seam down by a width equal to the fold area of your felling/lap foot. This will vary depending on your sewing machine foot. The foot I used to make the samples (at right) has a ⅜″ fold area, so that's the amount I trimmed from the top layer.

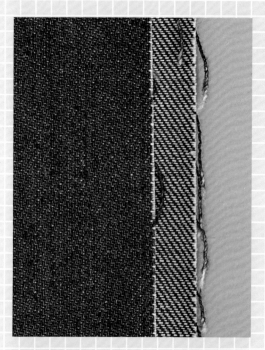

2. Set up the seam. Working with wrong sides together, lay the trimmed layer on top of the bottom layer, offset a bit to the left by the same amount you trimmed off, in this case that ⅜″. The extra fabric of the lower layer is going to be turned by the felling/lap foot and topstitched down.

3. Start stitching the first pass of the seam, feeding the edge of the lower layer into the foot. The foot will just fold over that extra fabric just once and will be easy to handle; just hold the fabric up a bit so it feeds naturally. Adjust the needle position to the left, if necessary, to make sure the line of stitching lands near the left cut edge. Some sewists go to the trouble of pressing the edge of the lower layer under first, but I don't. I actually find a pressed edge can interfere with the feed of the fabric into the foot. I trust the foot (you will, once you get the hang of it) to do an excellent job of folding the fabric over on its own.

4. Open up the seam and press it flat from the wrong side. Return to the machine and sew the second line of stitches, this time feeding the already folding edge through the foot, which will be even easier. Done. Now isn't that slick?

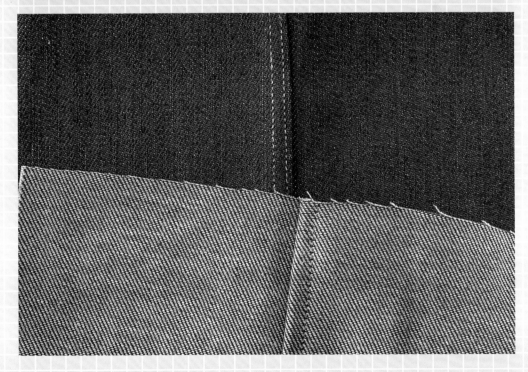

MINI LESSON

Installing an Invisible Zipper

Make it easy on yourself and invest in a decent invisible zipper foot. In my view, an invisible zipper is by far the easiest zipper to install. They are perfect for beginning sewists, as none of the stitching shows and they can be restitched as required to get it right.

I have sewn the zipper into this nice mint green fabric, stitching several times, in bright pink thread so you can see how much leeway you have.

1. Working from the right side of the fabric, before any part of the seam has been stitched, position one side of the open zipper facedown, zipper tape facing the cut edge of the pattern piece, the zipper teeth on the seamline. Pin the zipper tape into position, heads of the pins facing down so they can be removed as you sew.

2. Attach the invisible zipper foot. Unroll the teeth of the zipper slightly with your fingers to position the teeth in the groove on the underside of the foot closest to the cut edge.

3. Stitch one side of the zipper from the top to the bottom. Note the foot won't let you get all the way to the bottom of the zipper and the zipper stop; that's okay. Just stop stitching about 1″ or so before you reach the end of the zipper.

4. Close the zipper. Check to make sure your stitches are close enough to the teeth so the zipper tape doesn't show noticeably on the right side. Restitch, if necessary, moving the needle position over if that helps, until you are satisfied.

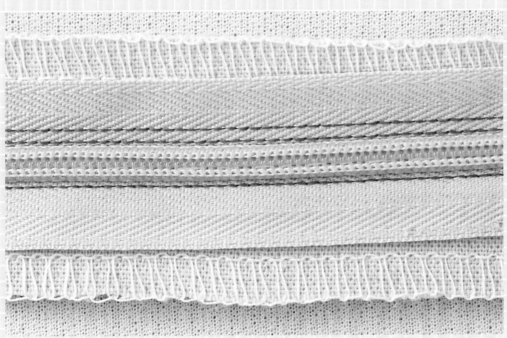

5. Stitch in the second side of the zipper.

6. Switch to a regular presser and, working from the hem up, sew the seam below the installed zipper closed. Don't try to connect the seam stitches to the zipper stitching; stop a little bit below, leaving a small gap that will be unnoticeable once the seam is pressed. Hold the ends of the zipper tape to the right to help you get close to the zipper stitching, switching to a regular zipper foot if necessary to do this.

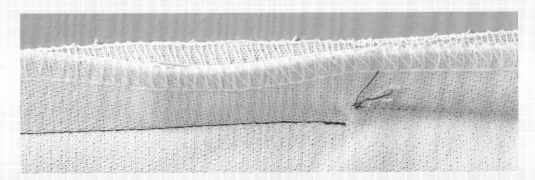

7. Turn and press from the right side, using a pressing cloth.

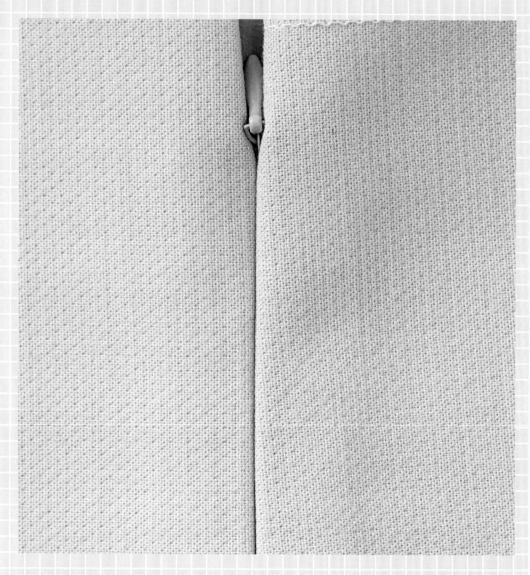

8. Tack the free ends of the zipper tape to the seam allowances on the inside with a few hand stitches to secure, if you wish.

Now why would anyone put in a dress or skirt zipper any other way?

NOW WHAT ABOUT A NEW MACHINE?

Sometimes, even once you really have mastered the machine you have, it becomes clear that you really need to trade up to get the results you want.

The truth is a machine that works with you rather than against you makes all the difference. But how to find a great sewing machine?

How to Shop for a New Machine

Here are some things to consider if you're thinking about a new machine:

⊗ Before you add that new machine to a virtual shopping cart, consider purchasing from a sewing machine dealer. It is important to make the most of what you buy. Look for a dealer who provides new-machine training sessions with the purchase, one who stocks a good supply of accessories, and one who offers classes. You want someone who is interested in education as well as sales. This is important.

⊗ If you have a tight budget, consider a second-hand machine from a dealer. Given a choice between that and a new *inexpensive* machine from a big box store or online seller, I would go for a dealer's serviced, reliable older machine every time. Also, if you buy a used or entry-level machine from a dealer, there is a good chance you will be able to trade in when you might decide to trade up. Relationships matter.

⊗ Take your own fabric when you go shopping. Sit at the machine and sew with fabric you commonly use. Never get up from test-driving a machine with having only sewn with "demo cloth" sometimes chosen to present the stitches well. It is also smart when shopping different brands to collect samples of common features—buttonholes, for example—so you can cross compare.

What to Look for in a New Sewing Machine

The next step is to figure out what you need to in a new machine. If you had me with you when you were machine shopping I would be on the lookout for the following features.

HAVE-TO-HAVES

Good buttonhole   Buttonhole disasters can ruin a garment. New machines often have all kinds of automatic, computerized, and special sensor-type buttonholes, but make sure you like the look of them. I would always make sure there is a manual option, too, that lets you control length, width, and size of cutting area. When assessing buttonholes, remember that any machine sews more efficiently forward than backward, so it is to be expected that the second side of any buttonhole worked this way looks a little different. This is also why buttonholes stitched with both sides in the same forward direction often look neater. The machines that can do this are either older and require you to rotate the garment for the second side of stitching, or they require the machine to straight stitch back to the beginning before the second side of the buttonhole is worked.

Knit buttonhole   Look for a buttonhole designed for knit fabrics, made with stretchy zigzag stitched sides, so it will stretch with and bounce back with the fabric.

Moveable needle position　This is terrific for edge stitching, zippers, and difficult to get at areas.

Adjustable stitch width as opposed to set zigzag widths. Satin stitching in particular is so much easier with a variable zigzag.

Feed dogs that drop easily　Lowering feed dogs is essential for free-motion quilting and sewing on buttons (yes, do them with a zigzag).

Three-step or multiple-step zigzag　I love this stitch for exercise wear, sewing in lingerie elastic, and for all exposed stitches on children's clothes—no long threads to get caught.

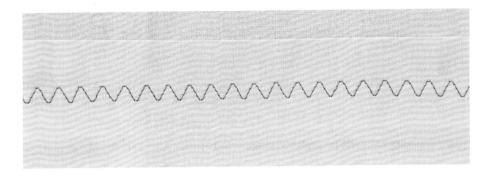

Built-in even-feed feature (a set of top feed dogs that can snap down behind the presser foot) **or a walking foot attachment** (page 156). So many sewing issues are solved by an even-feed system—consistent feeding of layers of any seam, stripe and pattern matching, control over slippery, napped or challenging fabric. In my world as a garment sewist, a walking foot or even-feed feature is an absolute necessity.

NICE-TO-HAVES

You can live without these features, but I warn you, once you get used to having them they can become must-haves.

Needle-down　Turn this on, and every time you stop sewing the needle will stay down in the fabric. This works like a third hand and is so nice when pivoting, rearranging the fabric, or doing some tricky stitching like sewing a stop-and-start curve.

Needle threader　This is a wonderful feature if you are into the progressive lenses, sewing late at night, or are just a sewing princess like me.

Low-bobbin thread indicator   How useful is this? Well just about as useful as a low gas light in the car.

Automatic tie-off or fastening stitch   This features eliminates the need for making a few stitches back and forth at the beginning and end of every seam. An excellent speed-demon feature.

Bar tack stitch   This stitch is awfully nice to have on automatic for the tops of patch pockets, the bottom of jeans zippers, and either ends of belt loops.

Darning stitch   This option is great for kids clothes and small holes in jeans.

COOL-TO-HAVES

These features make sewing easier, faster, and a little bit more fun.

Thread cutter   Of course, it's not hard to cut thread with scissors, but having that done for you makes sewing faster.

At least one simple, easy-to-read alphabet   Your kids don't lose things? You don't? If the machine lets you store words in a memory, you can do your own labeling.

Knee-operated presser foot lifter   My current BERNINA has one and I really find it useful. Being able to raise and lower the presser foot, particularly in combination with a needle-down feature, frees up your hands for more accurate sewing.

Extension table   This gives you an increased work area for larger projects, which is good for your accuracy, your comfort in front of the machine, and your nerves. Sometimes these come with the machine; more often they are available as an optional accessory.

Ability to wind the bobbin while you sew   Efficient people would wind a number of bobbins in advance. That's not me. I like to fill bobbins without interrupting my sewing.

DO YOU NEED A SERGER/OVERLOCKER?

If you don't have a serger and are considering one, I have one thought for you—don't be scared off by sergers and all those tension dials.

For some reason, many sewists fear tension. In fact, I once observed to a class that "nothing causes tension like tension," which at the time I felt was quite clever. It's true though. Most sewists attribute any stitch weirdness to tension issues because they don't know how else to describe them. Top-tension mechanisms in either a sewing machine or serger are actually quite simple, essentially tiny doll dinner plates that move closer or farther apart when the tension dial is turned, tightening or loosening the hold on a thread. This sort of control is necessary to regulate the speed with which thread is fed through the machine and a stitch is formed.

Sewists move tension dials all the time—loosening top tension to bury the lock-stitch to the underside in buttonholes and satin stitches, for example—and many of the newer machines even make these adjustments automatically.

The thing that makes many sewists nervous when they see sergers is that they have not just one tension dial, but three, four, five.... Not to worry. Sergers are actually mechanically simpler machines than sewing machines. Any direction in which any of those dials is turned, they can just as easily be turned back.

The numerous tension dials are not the only difference between these machines and a regular sewing machine. For a start, sergers (*overlockers* in most of the non–North American world) can both sew a seam and finish a seam at the same time. A blade trims the fabric before it passes under the needle, and two loops of thread, not surprisingly controlled by an upper and lower "looper," encase the seam allowances. All serged stitch variations—two, three, four, and five threads, as well as two- and three-thread rolled hems—are just variations on this mechanism, as altered by tension and threading changes and reconfigurations of the needles, loopers, stitch finger, and blade.

For a sewist used to working on a conventional machine, these differences on a serger are very obvious.

⊗ You don't have to raise the presser foot to start sewing. Extralong feed dogs pick up and move the fabric under the foot instead.

⊗ There is no reverse and consequently no forward and back at the beginning and end of every seam. In a serged seam, the thread ends are buried either by swinging the work around and serging over the thread tails again, by feeding the tails into a needle and burying under the looper threads, by touching with a liquid seam sealant, or by tying off manually, as I do. Seams that are crossed by other seams, of course, do not need to be secured at the ends.

⊗ A serger operates at high speed, at least twice as fast as sewing machine.

⊗ There isn't any bobbin.

⊗ The threading can be fairly complicated. In the old days, we did it often with tweezers and much angst, but it is much easier in the newer sergers. Most have built-in features to make threading easier; some even have automatic or air-propelled threading.

⊗ The feed dogs can be adjusted to operate at different speeds, a function not surprisingly called _differential feed_. This can stretch out thin fabrics that might pucker or hold back fabrics, like some knits, that can wave.

You might appreciate a serger for these reasons:

⊗ A serged seam stretches in a way a conventional machine lockstitch does not. This means you can serge through T-shirts, leggings, and bathing suits at top speed without any fear the seams will pop. You can also add a stretchy thread like a wooly nylon to the mix for particularly pro activewear.

⊗ Seam finishing is faster. I bought my first serger after spending five hours finishing the seams in an unlined jacket for my mom. Finishing the seam with a serger would have taken me about fifteen minutes.

⊗ You can reduce bulk with new construction techniques. Many edges you would turn under and stitch to finish can be simply serge finished. This can include the raw edges of facings, hems, and waistbands. I often replace back neck facings of blouses with a serged neck seam for a fast, easy finish, too. For those who might wonder if this is durable, at right is my first serged back neckline in a shirt, done 25 years ago and still going strong:

Common Serged Stitches

High-end sergers now have a wide variety of stitch possibilities, many of them with decorative potential. But if you plan to use your serger for sewing garments, the stitches you will use the most are the ones for serged seams, seam finishing, rolled hemming, and flat locking.

These stitches are the standards found on the most widely used two-, three-, and four-thread sergers.

Four-thread serged seam This functional stitch has two rows of needle stitching and an overcast edge. Since a serged seam is also a stretchy seam, this is the stitch used in most knit garment construction. Note, though, that the two fabric layers are overcast together. If you use a serger to sew wovens, you will not be able to press the seams open.

Three-thread serged seam This stitch is formed with only one, not two, needles and can be recognized by the single row of needle stitching and the overcast edge. In general garment construction this stitch is most often used to finish seams. Some sewists do this as they go, but many sewists serge-finish most of the raw edges of all pieces before they start to assemble a garment. Three-thread seams are particularly stretchy and often used in activewear.

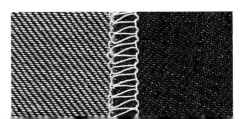

Three-thread rolled hem   Like the three-thread overlock, this stitch is made with one needle and two looper, overcasting threads. However, the serger's stitch finger is disengaged or replaced with a much narrower version, so the cut edge of the fabric is rolled under with the overcasting, much like is done in a hand-rolled hem. In the knit below, the fabric was stretched as it was fed to create a "lettuce" effect with the three-thread rolled hem.

Two-thread rolled hem   Lighter-weight, less-thread version of the three-thread rolled hem, often used in fine fabrics, such as the silk below.

Flatlock stitch   This is another variation of a three-thread seaming technique and is made by loosening the needle tension so much that the stitched seam can be pulled flat.

The absence of seam allowance bulk in flatlocking makes this a good stitch for close fitting garments, such as running leggings and bike shorts. The flatlock can be wide or narrow, depending on whether you use the right or left needle. Either side of the stitch can be used on the outer garment for different visual effect.

Here is a finished two-thread flatlock once the seam is spread from the top side, showing the loopers on the surface of the fabric.

And here is a look at the underside of the fabric once the seam has been spread, showing the ladderlike thread pattern.

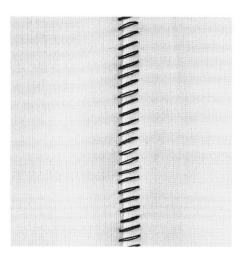

Chain Stitches and Coverhems

Another level of sergers (two-, three-, four-, five-thread) does the above stitches as well, but can also be converted to do chain stitches (think the sturdy stitching at the top of an onion bag).

Here is the chain stitch plus overlocked edge, an option you see in so much of ready-to-wear construction:

Additionally, many of the upper end sergers can be set up to do coverhems—the easily recognizable two rows of parallel stitching often used to hem knits, not unlike the effect of twin-needle stitching on a conventional machine. Depending on the machine, the coverhems can be made in variable widths and sometimes with three rows of top stitching.

Coverheming can also be done by dedicated coverhem machines. The dedicated machines are a popular option with two types of sewists: those who are happy with a standard serger but just want the hemming function and those who don't want to convert a more sophisticated serger to a coverhem every time they want to use this stitch.

Note that both the wrong and right side of a coverhem stitch can be used for different decorative effects. The two-needle coverhem is popular, but increasingly a three-needle coverhem, with three, *not two*, lines of stitching, is used to sew activewear. Here are the familiar parallel rows of topstitching on the top side of a two-needle coverhem stitch:

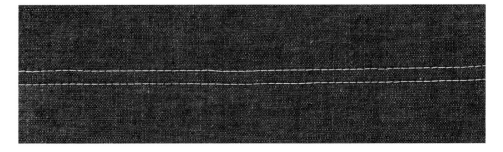

Here is the underneath of the coverhem, the side often seen in activewear construction:

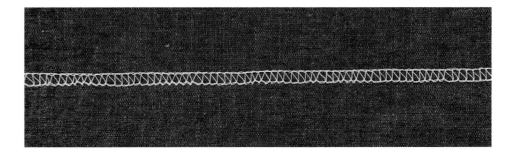

Serger Specialty Feet

Serger speciality feet are also interesting. The options available for your own serger are worth exploring. My favorite is the gathering or ruffling foot.

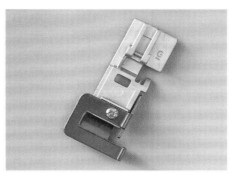

This foot takes advantage of the differential feed capacity of most current sergers. Differential feed is a serger function designed to eliminate puckers or waves in certain fabrics. Set higher, differential feed moves the serger feed dogs faster. By taking up slightly more fabric, it counters fabric waving in knits. Set lower, slowing the feed dogs, differential feed smooths out the puckers in fine fabric.

A serger gathering foot makes use of the ability to increase differential feed speed and amplifies it by increasing the pressure on the fabric over the feed dogs. So combined with an increased differential setting, a longer stitch length, and increased needle tension, this foot will produce miles and miles of finished even ruffles in minutes. Here's what that looks like:

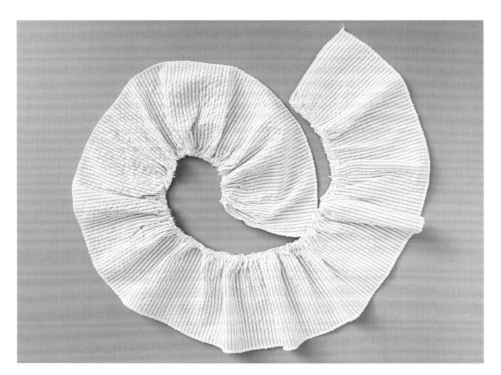

SEWING NOTIONS

Over the years I have probably bought nearly every nifty sewing notion invented. Below is an annotated short list of my favorites.

Threads

Yes, I consider thread a notion because the right one can make a real difference. The rule here is to match the fiber content and strength of the thread to the fabric—cotton for natural fabrics, polyester for synthetics or blends. Try not to mix types. Polyester threads in particular are notorious for working holes around the stitches in natural fabrics. I should add that I am not a fan of combo threads, such as cotton-wrapped polyester. I find the tougher polyester core eventually works its way through the cotton, splitting or unraveling thread on its way to a sewing machine needle—very discouraging.

SPECIALTY THREADS

Silk thread is great for basting and can be removed later without a trace. Silk also makes a lovely top-stitching thread, particularly in dressmaking.

Heavier top-stitching threads, provided they are used with a top-stitching needle, are essential for sturdy garments, such as jeans, outerwear, and bags. The color range of top-stitching threads can be limiting, however. If you can't find a good color in designated top-stitching thread for a fabric, try a reverse-action or triple straight stitch with the same thread with which you sewed the garment. That's how I top-stitched the mint green dress (page 86)—with two threads in a top-stitching needle. Any way you do it, know that the extra stitch definition can really finish a garment.

SPECIALTY SERGER THREADS

I have a couple favorite special-purpose threads that are particularly useful in garment construction. Both are most effective when used in a serger.

Fusible Thread

Generally off-white in color, fusible thread can be found on both spools and on cones. You can recognize it because it looks a lot like dental floss.

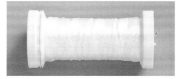

MINI LESSON

Prepare for Topstitching with Fusible Thread

In the serger, fusible thread behaves much like any other thread. But under the heat of an iron, it softens and adheres, hence its name. I love this thread and here's why.

Many new patterns, particularly those produced by indie designers, call for neckline and sleeve edges to be turned and topstitched. This is fine in principle but sometimes tricky to do without creating wrinkles or stretching out along the curved edges. Both these problems can be solved and eliminated with fusible thread.

1. Set up your serger for a wide or narrow three-thread overlock—the same stitch you use to finish seams. Thread the upper looper and needle with the usual thread, but put the fusible thread in the lower looper.

2. Serge finish the raw edges you intend to turn and topstitch.

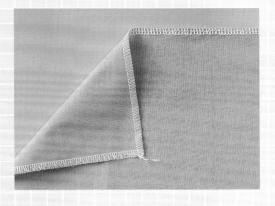

3. Take the garment to the ironing board and carefully press the edges under, using a pressing cloth to protect the iron. I find fusible thread goes into action at a moderate heat with a little steam. Work your way around the edge, lifting and pressing as you go. Try not to glide the iron.

Topstitch all edges in place from the right side. No pinning is necessary, of course. In addition to the time saved with this thread, I find that fusing the turned edge this way also adds stability to the edge and seems to prevent waving.

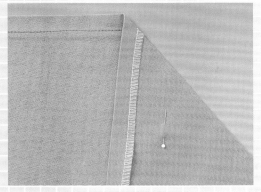

Now doesn't this just change your life?

Wooly Nylon Thread

Another highly useful serging thread is wooly nylon. This thread is sold on either midsize or large cones and can be identified by its fuzzy, almost yarnlike appearance when relaxed.

Wooly nylon thread has several really interesting characteristics. It is strong and for that reason is often used to sew activewear. It is soft, which makes it excellent for serge finishes and seams worn close to the body or next to sensitive skin—swimwear, lingerie, and baby clothes, for example. It has bounce and recovery. This makes it perfect for seams that need to stretch and not break, so it is often used in the bobbin for twin-needle top stitching and in the loopers and sometimes the needles when serging seams.

Handling wooly nylon thread can be tricky, but there are strategies that make it manageable.

First, because this thread can stretch thin and bounce back, I like to hand wind it onto a bobbin when I use it with twin needles. This hand winding helps the thread to feed smoothly at the machine and is worth the extra time it takes.

Second, trying to feed that fuzzy cut end into serger guides can be a challenge. However, if you just tie on a piece of regular sewing thread to the wooly nylon end, it can be fed through the machine quite easily. To thread the eye of a needle, use an old-fashioned needle threader. Most fabric stores carry them.

Adapting to this somewhat unusual thread is worthwhile.

MINI LESSON
Faux Binding with Wooly Nylon Thread

My own favorite use for wooly nylon thread is to use it to cover cut edges when serging for a soft, no-work version of an applied binding. This is a perfect finish for heavy knit edges, as a decorative substitute for a turned and stitched edge on a cardigan, for example, and to finish fleece scarves and baby blankets.

1. Set up the serger for a wide three-thread overlock. In most sergers this means using the *left needle*, not the right one. Put a sewing thread in the needle, but put wooly nylon in both the upper and lower loopers.

2. Set the stitch length to 1.0 or less, test the stitch, and adjust as necessary. The aim here is to have a balanced stitch, with the top and bottom loopers connecting nicely right on the cut edge. You may have to loosen or tighten one or both loopers to get this. Experiment until you are happy. Be aware that this thread will appear fine and thin under pressure but will spring back to its wooly state when released, which in this case is once it has been stitched in. You will find the fuzzies will fill in the spaces between stitches and this is what mimics the look of binding.

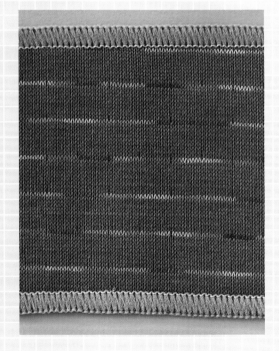

3. Serge around the raw edge. When you come to the end of the seam, try to overlap stitches, pivot the fabric away from the foot, and serge off. Cut the threads, dab the last few stitches with a seam sealant, and let dry.

Pretty cool, eh? Now think of all the ways you can use this thread and this technique.

Fine Pins

It breaks my heart when I see a new sewist struggling with short, blunt pins.

A thin, fine pin that just slips into the fabric is a must, the longer the better. I have recently become a fan of those fine flower-headed quilter's pins that are easy to see and remove as you sew.

Duckbill Scissors

The wide "duckbill" blade on the underside of these scissors prevents catching the underneath layer when a sewist trims. With a long history of mistake slicing, I like that kind of security. I also use regular sewing shears and some smaller thread snips.

Bamboo Point Press

A proper point turner/press is a necessity when turning anything with points, such as a collar. A bamboo one, unlike the plastic version, just feels right in a hand and you can even press over it.

Wire Loop Turner

Not all miracles are expensive. These units look like a long wire with a tiny latch hook at the end. Push this up into a tube, catch the latch in the seam allowance, and pull. Presto, a nice turned loop, no bleeding fingers.

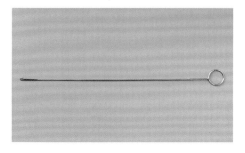

Masking Tape

Not a traditional sewing tool, but a wonderful one. I use pieces of masking tape to mark similar pieces and right and wrong sides of fabric, "left sleeve right side," for example. I also use it to mark placement lines on details that need to be even, such as the tops of patch pockets, and as a cutting guide when I have to cut same-size strips/bindings and can't find my rotary cutter. Masking tape is a real help when you have finished unpicking a million stitches—just press a length over the thread bits and lift them off when you pull away the tape.

Seam Ripper

Show my sewing protégé, my seven-year-old granddaughter, Scarlett, a seam ripper and she will tell you, "That's a sewist's best friend." (She has sewn with me a lot.) Ripping, unstitching, reverse sewing, whatever you call it, all sewists will at some point have to unpick a mistake and try again.

TIP The difference between a great sewist and an average sewist is a seam ripper.

A really good seam ripper has a nice full handle that feels comfortable in your hand and a fine really sharp point. The Alex Anderson 4-in-1 Essential Sewing Tool (by C&T Publishing) comes with a sharp seam ripper, stiletto, presser, and point turner.

The scalpel kind of seam ripper is useful, too, particularly for undoing serged seams. Just use the blade to cut through the loops and the needle thread and seam will release quite easily.

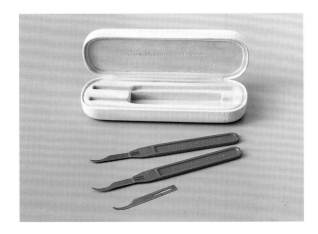

Barbara's Tips

✓ Bobbin Thread

- If you are lucky enough to have one of the new machines that has a low bobbin thread indicator, great. However, if you have an older, much-loved machine that does not, there is a great hack for that. When you wind bobbin thread, just make a little mark with a washable fabric marker on the thread about an arm's length before the cut end of the thread. When this bit of colored thread appears in your stitching you will know you have probably enough to finish the seam and no more.

- Be careful not to wind a bobbin too fast. This stretches a polyester thread that will later retract and distort the stitch.

✓ Choosing Thread Color

- If you are having trouble getting a good thread color match always go for the slightly darker rather than the slightly lighter thread. Threads always appear a little lighter once they are stitched in.

- When sewing a patterned fabric with several colors it can be hard to find a good thread match. In these situations I often put one dominant color in the top of the machine and another in the bobbin and have been happy with the results.

Oiling Your Machine

- Consult your owner's manual and oil a little but often, generally in places like the bobbin hook where metal moves against metal. Make sure you use a clear, fine, air-dissolving machine oil and never one of those handy dandy "all-purpose" lubricant that can gum up the machine.

- Your machine needs oil. But so often sewists don't like to oil because they fear stains on fabric. To prevent this, before you go back to stitching on fabric, make sure you sew up and down at least a yard of doubled paper towel after you oil.

Smart Seam Ripping

Learn to make the most of your seam ripper. Rather than painfully taking out mistakes stitch by stitch, use the point of the tool to cut every 4–5 top stitches. Then just pull on the bobbin thread and the entire seam should open up. Always press away the needle marks before you resew the seam.

Buttons

- It is important that any button floats on the surface of the fabric and doesn't pull in or pucker it. For this reason, heavy fabrics like coatings always use a button with a shank, either one that is part of the button or one you make with thread. To make a thread shank, lay a wooden matchstick (these have square sides and so don't shift while you work) underneath the button to elevate it while you sew. When the stitching is complete pull the matchstick free and wrap the thread shank several times with sewing thread to secure and fasten off.

- Absolutely nothing lifts the quality level of a garment more than good buttons. Some of the nicest clothes I own are ordinary thrift store finds that I just upgraded by removing the cheap plastic buttons and replacing them with buttons that were much more interesting.

 ## Choosing Stitch Length

Keep it all to scale. For the smoothest seams, use a shorter stitch length on thinner fabrics and a longer stitch length on heavier fabrics.

Fixing Thread Irregularities

If you notice irregularities in the looper threads in your serged edges, check to see if they seem to be occurring regularly, say every 1″–2″. If so, this is a sure indicator that the problem is how your threads are unwinding at high speeds. To fix this, change your threads to all the same kind (cones, for example) and make sure they are all unwinding in the same direction.

 ## Changing Needles

Change your needles every 4–5 hours of stitching. I also like to put a new needle in when I sew buttonholes to prevent skipped stitches in the satin-stitched sides.

 ## Perfect Seam Allowances

It is handy to have the seam allowance distance to the needle clearly marked on the throat plate, as this can vary. Use a moveable tape, such as Sewing Edge—Reusable Vinyl Stops for Your Machine (by C&T Publishing), to do that.

✔ *Pressing Napped Fabrics*

When pressing any fabric with a napped surface, cover your ironing board with a napped fabric, too, so the pile doesn't get flattened in the process. This padding can be a purchased "velvet board," a towel, or a scrap of the fabric being pressed itself (my favorite).

✔ *Cleaning Lint from Your Serger*

Over time, lint can get built up between the tension disks in your serger. When this happens, the disks have trouble closing in on the thread and the stitch can start to look loose. To fix this, try knotting a piece of dental floss and "floss" the disks out.

✔ *Clearing the Plate*

Although you don't have to bring up the thread from the bobbin in a serger, since there isn't any bobbin, you do have to "clear the plate" and pull all threads free, separate, and under and to the back of the foot before you start stitching to set up the stitch formation properly. If your serger thread repeatedly breaks after a few inches of sewing, this is a clear sign you need to do clear the plate.

✓ Which Elastic?

Elastic is more interesting than you think. I use three kinds. For general sewing, I use "braided" elastic, because you can stitch through it without losing the stretch. For children's clothes that are much laundered and for swimsuits, I use chlorine-proof elastic for durability. You will recognize it by its natural, muslin color. Finally, for many waistbands 1″–1½″ wide, I look for "nonroll" elastic, which has either ridges or little boxes knit in so it really won't fold and roll around your middle.

✓ Buttonholes in Knit Fabrics

- Stretch-stitch buttonholes are very helpful when sewing knit fabrics because they will stretch when used and bounce back to shape. If your machine doesn't have one of those, try stitching the buttonholes vertically with the direction of less stretch instead of horizontally.

- For knit buttonholes in heavier fabric, you also can sew the satin-stitch sides of the buttonhole over cording for the most stable buttonholes of all. To make a corded buttonhole, lay a loop of heavier thread under the buttonhole foot, catching it on the hook at the back of the foot, and let the machine stitch over the cord. Once the buttonhole is stitched, just pull the tails of the thread so the loop disappears and clip them off.

✓ Sewing Smooth Curves

When sewing around a curve, shorten the stitch length. This makes starting and stopping, while still maintaining an even curve, so much easier.

8 Mapping Out Your Own Sewing Strategy

Rules You Shouldn't Break   193

Sometimes the Best Advice Is Your Own   206

Barbara's Tips   223

MOST OF US LEARN TO SEW FROM READING PATTERN INSTRUCTIONS. This is a great place to start. But the truth is most instructions leave out a lot. Reading what to do next is not the same as knowing why you should do it or what happens if you don't.

The key to loving to sew is understanding the rules you should never break and identifying the ones that you can or even should break. And if you suspect there is an easier way to do something, there probably is.

So here we go.

Interfacing ... one more demonstration that it's what is inside that really counts.

RULES YOU SHOULDN'T BREAK

Grain

Grainline is everything. This is nonnegotiable.

All patterns include grainline arrows that must be aligned with the grain of fabric. Measure both ends of the grainline arrows on the pattern pieces to the selvage edges meticulously; it makes a difference.

However, knits being nonwoven fabrics don't have a real grainline. What they have instead, and just as essential to honor, is a direction of maximum stretch, running nearly all the time across the fabric from selvage to selvage. To make sure your clothes stretch where you do, make sure each pattern piece is laid out with the maximum stretch, also running across the pattern piece, such as armhole to armhole in a T-shirt front or side seam to side seam on pants.

Most good knit patterns have maximum stretch marked on them or direct you to lay out the pattern so all pieces will stretch most across the body. In any case, it is your job to make sure you place the straight of grain vertically for each pattern piece on woven fabrics and the greatest stretch horizontally for each pattern piece on knit fabrics. Garments that cut off grain or without considering maximum stretch will twist, hang oddly, stretch out of shape, or if they are knits will even be too tight to wear. None of it good.

Easy crossover V-neck (page 210)

Cocoon-shaped dress with a faced hem

Stay Stitching

Keeping the grain stable *during construction* is really important, too. Bias areas, both those that are cut that way and anything with a curve, can really distort when handled. A scoop neck that started out as a 20″ opening, if not staystitched, can quickly turn into a 23″ opening and leave a big gap at center front.

Definitely staystitch any curved area, as well as all seamlines, if the fabric you are using is a loose weave.

Always staystitch right after cutting out and before construction starts. The object is to stabilize vulnerable edges before they might be stretched out of shape by handling.

To staystitch, place a line of straight stitching just fractionally in from the seamline, working from wider garment area to narrower and up the garment and/or in to the center. For example, stitch from hem to waist in a skirt.

For a neckline, staystitch in two stages: from shoulder to center front in a neckline and then in from each side. Never try to staystitch continually around a neck opening; that will just push the grain off in one direction.

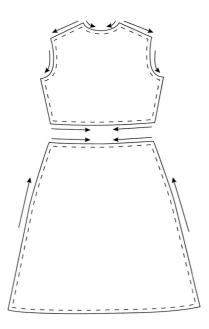

Turn of Cloth

This is such a simple idea. Fabric has dimension and this has to be allowed for it when dealing with layers. An example helps:

> Take the usual advice for applying a ¼″ bias trim to a neckline. The instructions say cut a bias strip 1″ wide and to sew it to the neckline with a ¼″ seam allowance. Theoretically this makes sense—stitch a ¼″ seam allowance, press it up a ¼″ to the cut edge, fold it over the top and down the other side ¼″, and then fold the raw edge under a ¼″ and topstitch it down.
>
> $4 \times ¼″ = 1″$ ... Right? ... *Wrong!*

In most cases, by the time that binding is wrapped to the wrong side, it is too short and frequently missed in topstitching.

The issue here is turn of cloth. The 3 layers of fabric in the first step of this process—garment, seam allowance, and binding—consume a considerable portion of that 1″, leaving you with too little to work with on the wrong side of the garment for the final topstitching.

See this one coming. In this case, cut the original binding 1½″ wide to accommodate turn of cloth and so your hands have something to work with. You can always trim off or fold under any excess on the wrong side if needed.

Look for turn of cloth and account for it.

TIP   When applying bias binding, take advantage of its malleability and press it to match the shape it has to fit before you attach it. For example, press the binding for a neckline into a curve. Ripple-free binding guaranteed!

Interfacing Even When Not Suggested

I think interfacing is really important. Just like a good bra and character, it is one more demonstration that it's what is inside that really counts. I find it helpful to use more than one kind of interfacing in a garment—crisp in a collar, softer in a front facing, and softer still within a hem—and to use far more interfacing and in more places than a pattern suggests.

> **TIP**   To interface a light fabric, say a collar or cuff in lawn, use silk organza. It adds opaque but effective support.

Add interfacing anywhere there is a detail to support or anywhere extra body might help the garment hang better. Interfacing types and how to apply them have been discussed (see Chapter 6: Choosing and Cutting Fabric, page 116).

Here are some areas where I typically add interfacing, making sure I trim the seam allowances away from all but the lightest interfacing to eliminate any extra bulk in the seam allowances:

Shoulder and waistline seams   I use fusible knit interfacing a lot. It adds little bulk and does not stretch along its length—useful when stabilizing weight-bearing seams. Just iron a strip onto the seam allowance.

Behind patch pockets   In any fabric heavier than a shirt weight, iron a square of fusible knit behind the pocket area on knit dress to prevent droopy pockets and a lightweight woven fusible (matching the characteristics of the interfacing to the fabric) behind any pocket treatment on a woven.

In seam allowances   Insert interfacing where a zipper will be inserted. This takes just a few seconds and keeps zippers neat and ripple free. Keep the interfacing light and match knit to knit, woven to woven.

Hemlines   Yes hemlines. Interface all but narrow hems, and interface both garment bottom hems and long- or three-quarter-length sleeve hems in any fabric heavier than a shirt fabric. Straight skirt hems in particular are improved by the structure of an interfaced hem. To avoid stiffening the hem, use either bias-cut wovens or a fusible knit.

Here I have interfaced the top hem of a linen patch pocket so it will stay flat against the jacket:

Additionally, a properly tailored coat always has a bias-cut interfaced hem of cotton or hair canvas. If the coat fabric is soft or napped, the hem can also be interfaced with bias cut flannel for support with softness.

Sleeve caps, entire jacket fronts, and between the shoulder blades of a jacket or coat back—all three of these areas benefit from interfacing to support multiple details, such as buttons, buttonholes, and pockets in the fronts. Interfacing keeps the fabric shape under strain in a jacket back or supports a line in a sleeve cap. This extra support can really save even casual jackets from a collapsed look. Always test the interfacing on a scrap first. If applying it to a partial area, trim the edge with pinking shears to blend it in.

Markings

Boring as markings are, they really represent an investment at the front end you can collect on all through construction.

The trick is to make markings that are meaningful. I use a personal code of clips in the seam allowances (a V-notch for fold line and a clip for any fold-to lines) and color-coded tailor tacks (yellow for darts, orange for pocket placement, and so on) for most of my other markings.

Make sure that markings you need to see from the right side are actually on the right side. To mark a patch pocket placement, use a tracing wheel and paper to mark the wrong side and then baste over this by hand to transfer the markings to the right side.

MINI LESSON
Easy Thread Marking

Thread marking is safe and it is accurate. I realize there are cool markers out there, but on this one I go old-school. Tailor tacks are fast to make and can be removed without any trace from any fabric. Here is how you make them.

Note: *These would be made right through the pattern tissue as required, with the paper gently torn away (use the sharp of your needle to make a tiny hole) when you are done.*

1. Use an unknotted doubled thread and take 1 small stitch through all layers.

2. Take another stitch over the last stitch and leave a loose loop about the size of your index finger.

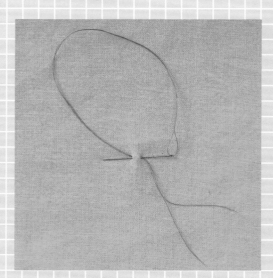

In effect, you are making a thread loop through your pattern/fabric that looks like a cursive "e." Cut the thread, leaving a few inches of thread tails at either end.

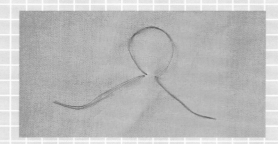

3. Don't cut the loop open. When you pull the layers apart to clip the threads, the intact loop will keep the thread markings from pulling out of the fabric.

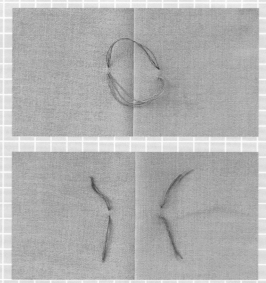

Reduced Bulk

The less going on behind the seams, the smoother the outside of any garment.

There are four ways to reduce bulk:

⊗ Whenever possible, clean finish (bind or serge) a raw edge rather than turning it under. Consider replacing facings on necklines and sleeveless armholes with binding.

⊗ Grade (meaning *trim*) seam allowances on edges so they aren't the same width. This prevents ridges showing through on the right side. When grading, always keep the seam allowance closest to the body narrower by at least ⅛″. When grading, remember that the shorter trimmed edge will always want to roll in. You can use this to your advantage in any jacket with a lapel that turns back. Create a natural break in the roll line by trimming the facing seam allowance shorter than the garment seam allowance up to the point where the lapel folds open, cutting right to the stitching line at this spot (the break point); then do a switch, trimming the garment seam allowance so it is shorter than the facing seam allowance.

⊗ Trim bravely, clip frequently. Cut open darts in heavy fabrics as far as possible before pressing open.

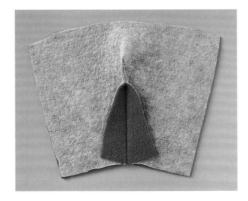

Stagger the clips and make them diagonal to minimize fraying, if that is a worry. To further minimize fraying, fuse a small square of interfacing at points where a single clip has to go. For example, place the square right to the stitch at the V in a V-neckline (page 210).

Also staystitch and clip frequently along any neck edge as often as necessary so it can be pulled straight enough to be stitched to a collar. The stay stitching will keep the clips from going any further than you need them. This is a great technique, as sewing two straight edges together is infinitely easier than trying to fit a curved shape to a straight one. Here is what that clipping can look like around the neck edge of a shirt:

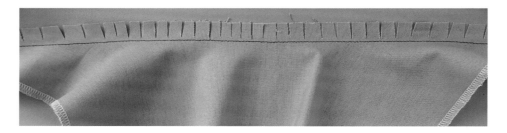

⊗ Learn how to notch. Notching removes extra fabric from convex (curved out) shapes so when they are turned right side out, they will lie nice and flat. This is a very useful technique when constructing the curved flap for a handbag or around a curved pocket, for example.

Pressing

Spend as much time at the ironing board as at the sewing machine.

The operative word here is press—up and down, *not a slide*—and don't move the fabric until it has cooled. This gives the press a chance to set.

Always protect the right side of the fabric with a pressing cloth. Avoid those sold as "pressing cloths," as they really are too heavy. Plain cotton broadcloth works fine, and silk organza yardage is even better because you can see through it, too.

Try not to let seam allowance bulk show. Press seams twice, once flat to imbed the stitches and then again open from the wrong side. Use a seam roll (page 149), which isolates pressing only on the stitching. Also, try not to flatten curved edges on an ironing board. Always press seams for darts, princess, and hip seams over a similarly curved edge, such as the end of seam roll or a ham (page 150).

The pressing rules for knits are different. With knits, less is more. Never press with the weight of the iron directly on the surface. In fact, I usually don't press my knits at all until construction is done; when I do, it's only carefully by eye, shooting in some steam and patting the fabric with my hand where I feel some smoothing would be helpful.

TIP

More knit garments are ruined by overpressing than any other technique. Remember, once you have overflattened or stretched out a knit with an iron, you just can't get the original shape back. Be cautious with instructions that suggest wovenlike press-as-you-sew instructions when working with knits.

If You Are Going to See It from the Right Side, Stitch It from the Right Side

Okay, so maybe this isn't really a universal sewing rule, but it is one of mine. No seam ever looks better once it is turned over, however nice that would be. Stitch from the side it will be seen—even if this means changing the construction steps. When given a choice between turning under the raw edge of the underside

of a cuff and machine stitching it down, hoping the stitches look fine from the right side, I would stitch the cuff to the sleeve, right side of cuff facing to wrong side of sleeve, fold the cuff to the right side, and then topstitch (page 248) *that* raw edge in place instead.

Have a Repertoire of Hand-Sewing Stitches

Hand stitching gives you control. For example, instead of stitching and turning a facing at the bottom of a jacket, I press under both seam allowances and stitch facing to hem by hand from the right side, allowing me to adjust this short connecting seam so it won't pull or pucker. Here are some of my favorite hand stitches:

Slip stitch   Sewn right to left for right-handers (hide the needle under the fold, and the traveling thread will also be minimized), the slip stitch is a good all-purpose construction stitch.

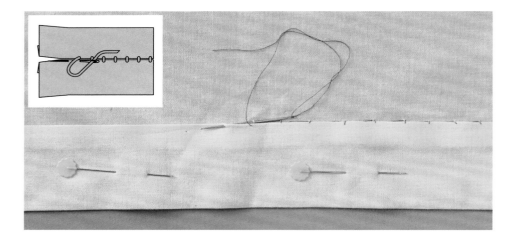

Catch stitch   Sewn in the opposite direction, left to right for right-handed sewists, a herringbone stitch like all zigzag stitches is flexible and therefore suitable for hems, including in knits and places where movement is useful like tacking down facings.

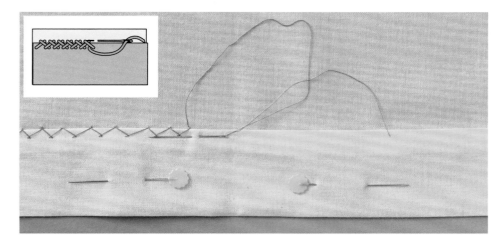

Backstitch   This stitch is handy as a strong hand stitch and useful in setting in a zipper by hand—a technique that actually can be easier than putting in a zipper by machine, particularly in tricky fabrics, such as velvet and satin. A mini backstitch like this, where the top stitch is smaller than the underneath stitch, is actually called a *prick stitch*—self-explanatory.

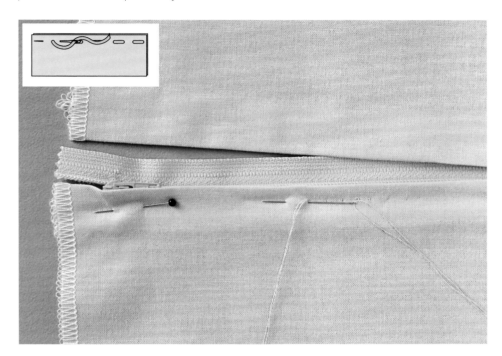

HAND STITCHES ON GARMENT EXTERIORS

Don't make the mistake of thinking that hand stitching has to be saved for interior finishing work.

The combination of durability and invisibility of handwork has been traditionally used by dressmakers for generations on external details, when it is often easier to do so than sew them on by machine. Some tailored patch pockets fall into this category. One of my favorite techniques is using hand stitching when I have to attach a pocket to a lofty fabric.

MINI LESSON
The Doubled Patch Pocket

Many patterns for coats or jackets call for patch pockets. These can be difficult to apply neatly by machine to heavier coating fabrics, such as melton, wool flannels, or mohair, due to the layers of thick fabric. Outerwear patch pockets can also go baggy over time—these are exactly the kind of pockets we all stuff with our hands, spare gloves, or dog leashes—and some sewists avoid them entirely for that reason.

You don't have to be that sewist. It is entirely possible to sew on a patch pocket in heavy fabric easily and in a way that will keep it flat and close to the body no matter how much wear the pocket gets.

The trick is to essentially attach two pockets: an inner sturdy one to take all the strain and a second, more elegant pocket laid over the working pocket. The latter one more for show and less for use.

1. Cut out the pocket pieces from coating fabric according to your pattern. Interface the top 1″–2″ edge of each pocket for support.

2. Press under all seam allowances on the sides and bottom of the pocket piece.

3. Mark the pocket placement on the garment front with markings that can be seen from the right side. I suggest tailor tacks or thread basting lines.

4. Stitch a rectangle of a sturdy lining fabric to the top of the pocket, right sides together. Make the pocket lining out of something durable, such as a cotton broadcloth or an outerwear fabric. Do not use a light dressmaking lining fabric for this job.

5. Position the lining section of the pocket unit on the front of the garment over the markings, right side to right side, with the pocket lining situated a hem-width distance below the top pocket markings. Pin the lining in place.

6. Flip the pressed pocket piece down over the lining and trace the shape onto the lining. You can see this done on the sample in a pink marker. Once marked, flip the pocket piece back up.

7. Stitch the pocket shape through the coating and lining layers with a small, close zigzag. Situate the stitches just inside the marked pocket line you just traced onto the lining. Take care to stitch through the lining and coat fabric. Stop stitching before you hit the seam that attaches the lining to the exterior pocket.

Note: At this stage, I also tend to round the corners of a square pocket shape in the lining, because I don't like crumb catchers in my pockets.

8. Closely trim extra lining fabric away from the line of stitching.

9. Fold the "real" pocket down to cover the inner lining pocket and pin in place. Make sure that all pocket seam allowances are tucked in and that they cover the lining edges well.

10. Hand stitch the edges of the pocket securely to the garment with a slip stitch, buried close to the edge so it is undetectable. This is so much easier and more elegant than machine stitching and just as strong.

That's it.

So easy, and since the stress of the pocket will be absorbed by the inner lining, this graceful outer pocket will still wear very well.

SOMETIMES THE BEST ADVICE IS YOUR OWN

After a long list of rules that can't be broken, you might be relieved to know there is a lot of room in sewing for your own ideas. So often the guide sheet method is not the only way or the best way.

Think for yourself. This translates to seeing issues that could be difficult and figuring out how to head off trouble before you get there.

Use your hands and use your head.

How do you solve your own construction problems? How do you find your own rules for sewing? Here are my tactics.

Feel Your Way

Arrange with your hands first and then sew. *To get it right, it has to make sense.* Lay out a complicated detail, fold under the seam allowances, see how the end product should look, and then walk the process back. See if you can identify an easier way to achieve the result.

Stand Back

Answer the why and you can figure out the how. Once I understood that a back neck facing was designed essentially only to cover a back neck seam, I ditched those awkward interfaced units and started binding or serging that seam instead for smoother, faster, harder-wearing results.

In the same way, when I figured out the secret to easing in sleeves was just to measure the arm opening and then adjust the gathers to this measurement, rather than pin-adjusting the sleeve into the armhole, my sleeve setting really improved. Then when I started to steam those sleeve caps into shape, hanging them over the end of the ironing board like a shoulder, *before I set them in*, my sleeves became near perfect. Sometimes new rules are made by breaking old ones.

Note that the pressing cloth I would normally use here between the iron and the sleeve has been removed to show the cap easing.

Use Your Critical Thinking Skills

Take one long ambitious seam and break it down into several sections. A bag pattern I recently used suggested basting in a zipper, exterior fabric, and lining, and joining them all together with one row of top stitching. Oh, my nerves! Instead, a sensible person should sew in the zipper to the exterior fabric, and then stitch on the lining using the existing line of stitching as a guide, turn, press, and finally topstitch. More steps, but each of them easy to do, with the same end result. Just like life, sewing taken in smaller steps makes everything more manageable.

Another example. Patterns often tell you to stitch to the clip. Why? This can be really hard to do when it all disappears under a presser foot and moving needle. Why not clip to the stitch instead? You have more control. Sew to the point of the clip, raise your presser foot with the needle down, and then use small scissors to clip right to the last stitch. Lower the presser foot and carry on. So much easier and the end results are identical.

Question the Conventions

Ask yourself: Why? What's the purpose?

Take facings. Why do we have them? In many cases, they are added to garment patterns to finish an edge. Sometimes this makes sense. Some fabrics need body around a neckline to hold the shape; I get that. However, it makes sense to look for opportunities to smooth things over and lighten things up.

Sometimes it even makes sense to leave off the facings entirely. One of the marks of couture sewing is its light hand in construction, and we can learn from that. As in couture, I often replace facings with bindings, and I am always pleased with the results.

In this camp shirt (page 228), I replaced a back neck facing with a bound seam.

I used bias binding instead of a bulky facing around the arm of a sleeveless blouse (page 15). This makes the shirt so much more comfortable to wear, too.

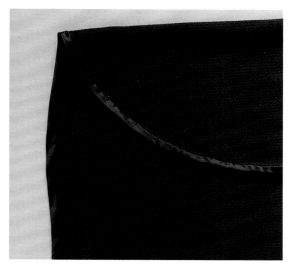

The pattern for this vintage cocktail dress (page 253) suggested both armhole facings and a fully faced hem. Since the wrap-around design of this dress required three armholes and a double layer in some areas of the dress, as well as a back overlay that could flip out when I walked, I was very wary of all that extra (and interfaced) bulk. Replacing all those facings with bias binding really helps this dress hang nicely and feel light when I wear it.

You have a choice on how you actually stitch a binding to an edge, depending on how you like to sew. I generally stitch the binding on right sides together, and then turn it to the wrong side and slipstitch in place. I used this method for the navy cocktail dress (page 22). Alternatively, you can stitch the binding on the inside the garment (right side of binding to wrong side of garment), and then flip it to the right side, turn the raw edge of the binding under and use a machine to topstitch it in place. I used this method on the striped top (page 14).

Putting Your Own Rules into Practice

To help you see what playing by your own rules looks like, I would like to share with you a few of the techniques I use when I sew for myself as substitute/alternative construction methods to the advice given in the pattern guide sheet.

Then it's over to you. Let's see how you can work through your own sewing challenges with a little confident problem-solving. You are better at this than you think.

MINI LESSON

A DIY Crossover V-Neckline

This is the method I used to sew the V-neckline featured in the striped knit dress (page 192). This crossover technique is a good alternative when you don't want to fiddle with a mitered V and is totally fool proof—there are no surprises. What you set up with your hands before stitching is what you will end up with.

1. Cut the binding twice as wide as you want to finished neck finish to be (you are going to be folding it in half), plus 2 small seam allowances (I use ¼″ seam allowances). Cut it a lot longer than you need. You can cut the extra off later and it is useful to have something your hands can hold onto during construction.

2. Iron a small piece of fusible interfacing to the wrong side of the neckline below the point of the V. *Do not staystitch.* If some of your stay stitches show and you try to take them out later, you will make a hole. The interfacing patch will provide all the stabilization you need.

3. Pin the binding around the neckline evenly along the long side of the V and stretched slightly across the back of the neck so it will hug the neck.

Note: The pinning and first pass of stitching should end several inches above the point of the V on the left side. Exactly how far away this stops doesn't matter; it just needs to be a fair bit longer than the width of the band. I think I stopped pinning and sewing about 2½″ before the point of the V to accommodate a band that was about 1″ wide. I eyeball this.

4. Stitch around the neck edge, starting a seam allowance distance below the V on the right side and ending somewhere short of the V on the left side where the pinning stopped in the example (at right). Use a straight stitch and a knit/ballpoint/jersey needle. As this is a V-neck and doesn't have to be stretched to go over your head, a straight stitch is just fine.

Clip right to the stitching at the point of the V.

5. Working from the right side, play around with the ends of the band so it looks like the example (at right) and pin in position. To arrange the V, just fold under the seam allowances on the unstitched section on the left side, tuck the right band into the opening there, and then tuck the long remaining part of the left band under the right. Pin in position from the right side to secure.

Note: If you have a pucker at the point of the V, that just means you haven't clipped right to the stitching. Go back and do that fearlessly. Remember you have interfaced this area.

6. Working from the wrong side, stitch the gap on the left side closed. Just continue that seam through all layers until the stitching meets the point of the V on the right side where the seam started.

7. To finish, trim off any extra tails from the binding, tack the left end to the right seam allowance, by hand or in this case by machine.

And the finished neckline is complete.

As a final step, you can zigzag the layers of the seam allowance together to flatten and then neatly trim away any excess seam allowance.

Pretty neat, eh?

MINI LESSON
Two DIY Elastic Waist Casings

I also almost always use my own method for making casings for elastic waistlines in pants and skirts. Here are two methods I use most often: the first for a finish that looks more like a real waistband than a casing and the second for close-body garments where I need the elastic to really stay put. *Note:* Neither approach requires any changes to the pattern pieces—the difference between these methods and what the pattern might suggest are only in the construction techniques. Fast and foolproof, I find both these methods give a more professional result than the more traditional approaches I'd used for years and for that reason are worth sharing.

FAUX WAISTBAND FOR KNIT OR WOVEN FABRICS

Sometimes the line of machine stitching left by a standard waistline casing can look a little casual or interrupt the look of an otherwise smooth garment. Close-fitting stretch-woven pants are a case in point. Many sewists who wear tops tucked still want a tailored looking waistband that feels as comfortable as any elastic waist.

Here is exactly how you can do that—an easy method that produces the look of a separate sewn-on waistband with only one row of stitching. Essentially, it is all in the folds.

1. Make the first fold. Fold the top of the garment down at the fold line to the inside of the garment, just as you would if sewing the usual casing. The wrong sides of the fabric will be together.

2. Make the second fold. Fold the whole casing you have just made down again, but this time to the right side of the garment. The first fold will then face down and the cut edge of the fabric will be even with the second fold, giving you three layers of fabric.

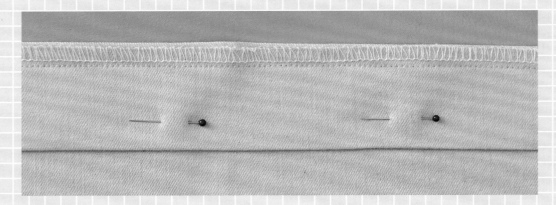

3. Stitch around this new fold at the top of the garment, ¼˝ from the top edge through all three layers, leaving a gap in the stitching as you normally would to feed the elastic through.

4. Flip this casing up and press. Note that there isn't any stitching showing on the right side. In fact, the casing now looks like a proper waistband. Insert the elastic to fit, and then join and close the gap in the stitching by machine.

Now how slick is that?

STITCHED-DOWN ELASTIC WAIST FOR KNIT FABRICS

A complaint folks have about elastic or pull-on waistbands is that the elastic can twist, can fold over, or that all the gathers of the garment can bunch up in one area—over a hip or a belly, for example. The most effective fix for all these issues is to stitch the elastic to the garment rather than trusting it to a casing where it can scoot around as you move. Note also that active wear, or garments that need to be worn close to the body, such as leggings, will feel and look much smoother and more like ready-to-wear if the elastic is stitched in.

1. Cut the elastic to fit your waist comfortably with some real snap to it when you pull on it and let it go. Remember that stitching will reduce the stretch in any elastic.

2. Sew the length of elastic into a ring. To avoid a lumpy join, don't overlap the ends. Instead, butt them together. To do this, zigzag one end of the elastic to a small piece of woven fabric and then place the other end right up next to it, cut edge to cut edge. Zigzag the second end of the elastic to the fabric. The extra woven can be trimmed away.

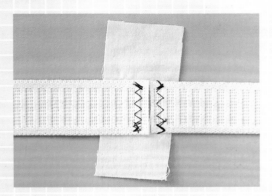

3. Try on the ring of elastic and see how it feels. Adjust if necessary. I usually even try to make the ring of elastic slightly tighter at this point than I might want it to feel when finished. The stitching on process invariably does loosen the elastic slightly and it is smart to allow for that.

4. Divide the garment opening into quarters and mark these quarter points with pins. Do the same to the ring of elastic. This is a technique called PMIQ (pin and mark in quarters) and is a classic way of dividing and applying any smaller unit so it fits evenly into a larger opening, whether it's elastic into a waistline as described here or a neckband into a neckline. To find the quarter points without getting out a measuring tape, simply fold both the waist opening and ring of the elastic in half and mark the folds with pins. Next, match the pins and fold again, and then mark those folds with pins

5. Pin the elastic to the inside of the garment, matching quarter pins, with the edge of the elastic about a ¼˝ below the edge of the fabric. Note that the elastic will invariably be smaller than the garment opening. Don't worry about that. You will stretch the elastic to fit when you stitch it in.

6. Using a medium to large zigzag stitch and sew along the bottom of the elastic to attach it to the opening, working from quarter point to quarter point. Stretch the elastic to fit the opening, but be careful not to stretch the garment fabric. Stop frequently to be sure you don't lose control; don't try to do it all in one go.

Note: Where you put this line of stitching is highly counterintuitive, since you sew along the bottom edge of the elastic. Trust me, this will make sense later. Also know that this first line of stitching will not show on the outside once the casing has been turned over. So don't worry at all if your stitching looks crooked in places as you stretch the elastic to fit the waist opening.

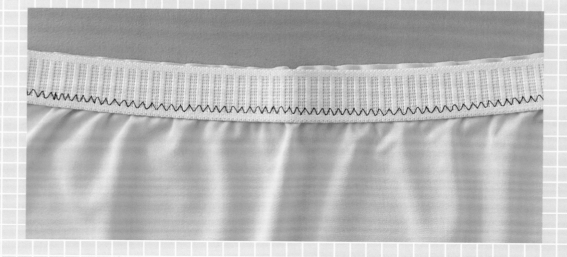

7. Fold the elastic down to the wrong side of the garment, encasing it in fabric. You will be interested to see that the first line of stitching you made on the bottom of the elastic is now at the top of the casing. Pin in place.

8. Working from the right side of the fabric, sew the bottom of the elastic to the garment through all layers with a stretchy stitch—either a plain zigzag, a three-step zigzag, or with a twin-needle or coverhem.

And you are done—a nice elastic waistline that will not shift, bend or bunch up and is securely attached in two places.

MINI LESSON

Two DIY Knit Necklines

The complaints I hear most often from new and returning sewists about the knit tops they make is that the necklines seem too loose, stand up too much, or just don't hug their necks neatly.

In my own view, it is pretty much impossible for any pattern maker to design a pattern piece for a knit neckline that can accurately work with the wide variety of knit fabrics a sewist can use. For this reason, I rarely use the neckband pattern pieces that come in the envelope. I use my own judgment and a few reliable guidelines to come up with my own neckline treatments.

Here are two ways of finishing a knit neckline that I use with good results, often substituting either of these methods for ones that may be suggested in the patterns.

INFORMAL KNIT NECKLINE

This is the most informal treatment and suitable for T-shirts, tops, and dresses. The neck can be finished this way with either the same knit as the garment (self fabric) or even a ribbing. It is so easy to do.

Setup: Sew the garment shoulder seams but not the side seams. Measure the size of the neck opening.

1. Cut the neckband. I always do this myself from my own calculations rather than use any included pattern piece. The reason for this is that different knit fabrics can have different degrees of stretch. I like to customize my binding length so it is just the right degree of smaller than the neck opening so it can hug the neck nicely and lie flat. Cut the band strip as wide as you want the finished neckband to be, plus 2 seam allowances—a 1″ finished band sewn with a ¼″ seam allowance would mean a strip cut 2½″ wide.

2. Calculate the length of the band; this will vary depending on the fabric. If working with self-fabric of moderate stretch, cut the length of the band three-quarters of the measurement of the neck opening plus seam allowances. If working with a very stretchy fabric or ribbing, cut the length of the band two-thirds of the measurement of the opening plus 2 seam allowances.

As an example, for a ribbing neckline 24″ in width, I would cut a neckband 16″ long (24″ × ⅔ = 16″) plus 2 seam allowances. However, if using the garment fabric itself, I would cut the neckband 18″ long (24″ × ¾ = 18″) plus 2 seam allowances.

Note: These ratios are pretty accurate. However, always remember every knit fabric has a unique degree of stretch—some more stretchy, others less so. So at this point I always double-check myself. I pin the short ends of the band together and see how it fits inside the neck opening. I need it to be just that bit smaller than the opening so it can stretch to fit, but not strain; stretch to fit, but not be too loose. The band should also have a natural inward curve to it, so it will cup the neck slightly when worn and not stand away from the body.

3. Stitch the short ends of the band together, and then fold the band in half.

4. Mark both the neckband and the neck opening at quarter points, using pins for these markings using the PMIQ technique (page 215) for the stitched-on elastic waistline.

5. Pin the neckband into the neck opening, raw edges and right sides together, matching the pins so the smaller band is evenly distributed within the neck opening.

6. Stitch the band in, stretching it to fit between the pins, taking care to stretch the band and not the opening. Use either a serger or a regular sewing machine set at a very narrow zigzag to do this. I find that the best way to do this is to stop-and-start sew, working from quarter mark to quarter mark and repositioning your upper hand carefully to make sure you are holding the band separately as you stitch.

Done. Very pro looking, isn't it?

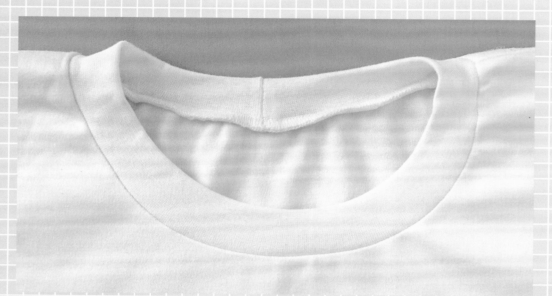

Note: Many instructions tell you at this point to topstitch the seam allowance down to secure it. I rarely do this. First, this seam allowance will turn down and to the inside naturally when worn because the band has been cut to be slightly smaller than the neck opening. Second, I find that straight stitches, especially in an area where the garment will have to be stretched every time you put it on, will tend to break over time. However, if you really decide you like the look of top stitching around the edges of the band, use either a twin needle (page 159) or a coverhem stitch (page 176), both of which provide stitches that stretch.

Also if you decide to press, do so by shooting some steam around the neckline and patting it with your hand. Keep this "pressing" on the garment. Never ever press the band itself, most particularly if it is made of ribbing. Once stretched out with an iron, the shape can never be recaptured.

DOUBLE-BOUND EDGE NECKLINE

This second method of finishing a neckline is slightly finer and may look more like ready-to-wear to you, as it has the appearance more like a binding than a sportswear band. *Note:* This technique produces four narrow layers of fabric around the neckline, so it is essential that you use this technique only on a garment made of a fairly thin fabric—a single knit or mesh knit, for example; nothing too heavy. Also be aware that this treatment does require some straight-stitch top stitching. To avoid stretching and breaking the line of stitching, use the top stitching only on wider round or scoop necklines where stretching the garment over your head as you dress will not be an issue.

1. Decide on the band width. *Note:* The finished width of the binding will not be as wide as the band above: a band cut 2½˝ wide will produce a binding of about ½˝–¾˝ depending on turn of cloth. If you are using self-fabric, cut the length of the band three-quarters of the size of the neck opening and test it for fit before you stitch.

2. Sew the short edges of the band together and fold in half lengthwise, wrong sides together. Using the PMIQ technique (page 215), pin the circle of binding to the neck opening of the garment evenly, but pin it with the right side of the band to the wrong side of the garment. It will look very much like the ring of ribbing pictured in the first neck treatment, except that this time it is pinned inside the garment and not on the outside.

3. Sew the band on. To reduce bulk, I always do this with a narrow zigzag on a regular sewing machine rather than a thread-heavy serger stitch.

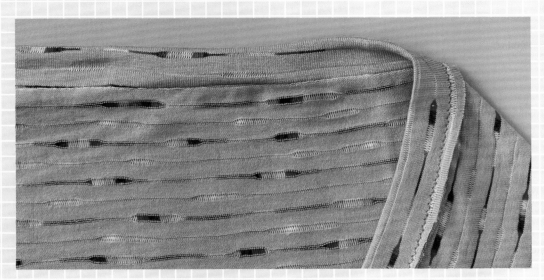

4. Once the band has been stitched on, flip it to the right side and pin it in place around the neckline. Topstitch the folded edge of the band as evenly as you can to the neckline—an edge-stitching foot or a zipper foot is a huge help here.

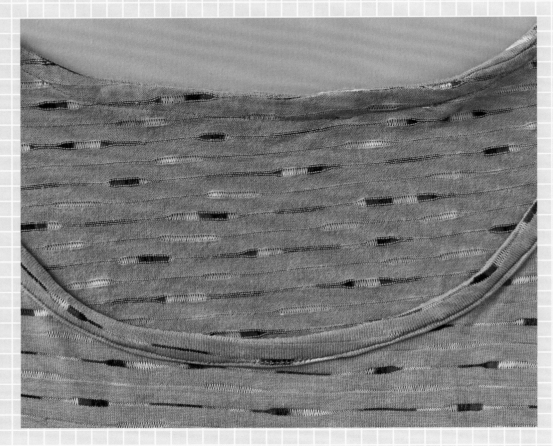

Nice and neat, both inside and out.

Barbara's Tips

✓ Better Hems

- The narrower the skirt, the wider the hem. For a straight skirt, try a 2″–2½″ hem; an A-line skirt 1½″; a very full skirt ⅝″–¼″.

- Let garments hang before hemming—overnight for a straight skirt or dress, a full day for an A-line, and a day and a half for a very full or bias garment. Then recheck the hem level when worn and trim a bit if necessary.

- Press a hem only along the fold. Pressing the whole hem creates a ridge.

- Hand stitch a metal chain (Coco Chanel–style), often sold in fabric stores by the yard for handbag handles, to the hemline of a knit cardigan to keep it from riding up at the back.

✓ Better Buttonholes

For better machine buttonholes, put in a new needle to prevent skipped stitches, loosen the upper tension so the lockstitch stays on the wrong side, use a stabilizer under thinner fabrics, and use a cotton machine embroidery thread for the smoothest look. The little fuzziness of this thread will fill in the satin stitches.

Better Buttonholes continued

- Draw your buttonhole markings on a long piece of masking tape and place it vertically near the center front of a shirt or blouse as a stitching guide. These strips of tape can be saved and reused for the next project.

✓ Better Cutting

If you are frustrated with your own messy cut edges, try cutting with the pattern piece to the right of the scissors (or to the left if you are left-handed). To do this, you may have to rough cut the pinned fabric into sections so you can turn each piece as you cut. But the neatness of the cut makes this extra effort worthwhile.

✓ Better Top Stitching

Don't fall into the trap of thinking a presser-foot distance is a standard stitching guide. In top stitching, both the stitch length and the distance from the edge need to reflect the thickness of the fabric. A thinner fabric will look best topstitched with an average stitch length near the fold. A thicker fabric should be topstitched with a longer stitch length and ¼″ or more away from the fold.

✓ Hand Stitching

- If your hand sewing thread always knots up, try running it over a dry bar of soap a few times to smooth the little fibers that catch. You can also use beeswax, of course, but most of us don't have that handy.

Hand Stitching continued

- When hand stitching a hem, place the pins on the outside of the garment. This way, the thread won't get caught on the pins while you work.

- The finer the hand sewing needle, the smaller your stitches will be. Large needles pick up more fabric threads, thinner needles pick up far fewer.

✔ Ripple-Free Pressing

- Always press in the direction of the grain, lifting and pressing as you work your way up the seam. The same rules apply here as apply to stay stitching (page 194): Press from widest to narrow—up from the hem of an A-line skirt toward the waist, for example, or in to the center front of a neckline in two presses from the shoulder neck edge. You will be amazed at how much better your garments will hang if you do this.

- Always press horizontal darts down and vertical darts in, toward center front or center back.

✔ Easy Gathers

I rarely use the usual rows of long stitches to gather a major edge, along the waist of a gathered skirt for instance. Instead, I just lay some heavier thread, such as a top-stitching thread, on the fabric and just zigzag over it. The zigzag stitches act like a casing and the cord can be easily pulled to make fast gathers.

Sewing for Joy

YOU HAVE BEEN IN MY MIND AS I HAVE WRITTEN THIS BOOK.
I have thought of young sewists who know they could make something so much better for less. I have identified with parents sewing late at night when the kids are in bed—or during the day in snippets of time when little ones are taking naps. I have seen working persons, like so many I have taught, who decide to do something for themselves and take a class. And I considered the returning sewists getting back into activities they once enjoyed. I hope something in what I have shared here has been helpful to each of you.

I think sewing needs to be always something you choose to do because it adds joy to your life. Whatever you do, however much you want to improve your skills, perhaps even by reading books like this, be careful never to let it become just one more obligation. However proficient or productive you become, always make sure you are having fun. Here are ways you can do that.

Put your self-imposed sewing pressures into perspective. You're doing just fine. Enough is a concept to be considered.

Applied slant pockets

Chambray shorts

Waist casing faced with same fabric as shirt

Sew Only What You Really Enjoy Making

Make sure you never sacrifice enjoyment in your sewing. Even if every other blogging sewist on the internet is sewing 57-piece trench coats, if that doesn't blow your hair back as my husband would say, don't feel you have to do it, too. Don't take it all too seriously. Too many of us do—sewing just to keep up with the sew-alongs, to feed the blog, to display up to Instagram, or to have something to share on other social media. Listen, if you find yourself intimidated by the blogosphere or Pinterest, I have one number for you: *7.5 billion*. That's the number of folks on this planet right now. Put your self-imposed sewing pressures into perspective. You're doing just fine. Enough is a concept to be considered.

Let me tell you a story. My sewing friend Trudy and I sew together many Saturdays. A while ago, after a great T-shirt production day, we looked at each other and said, "From now on we're only going to sew knits for ourselves." We have only partially stuck to this plan, but the point is that that's the day we made this decision. Then we sat there. And you know what happened? Nothing. We were allowed. Sometimes deciding what you are not going to do is as inspiring as what you do.

Limits are actually pretty interesting and are often quite liberating. Figure out what kind of sewing feels like duty to you and ditch it. Sew for kicks.

Which brings me to creativity.

Back neck edge is bound.

Convertible collar

Motifs on packet match up with shirt

Retro style camp shirt

Keep It Creative

It just breaks my heart when some woman says to me she isn't creative. Who told her that? I just *know* everyone is creative; I have simply seen the evidence, over and over again. The trick is not to find out if you are creative. The trick is to find your own personal door into your own creativity. Find your door.

How do you do that? A good way to start is to impose some boundaries on your sewing and see what happens next. When there are edges to what you can work with, you *have* to be ingenious, and ingenuity leads to true creativity. What particular limit brings this out in you is personal. Maybe repurposing rather than sewing new will get you cooking. Perhaps seeing how many different ways you can use the same pattern will bring out your inner inventor. The longer I sew, the smaller the number of patterns in my rotation but the more I do with them. Fewer choices, as Depression-era quilts show so well, nurtures creativity and, it turns out, creators.

Expand Your Scope

It is also important to keep trying something new. Of course, there is pleasure in doing what you know how to do well. But there is a special satisfaction in conquering a new challenge. That's the stuff that really makes you proud of yourself, and who doesn't need some more of that?

Let me tell you another story. A long time ago I had a phobia about bound buttonholes. I tried and I tried. Every method, every trick. Finally I found a way that worked for me ... that worked for my hands. One day, when the baby was sleeping, I made a bound buttonhole in silk jersey no less. And you know what? It was perfect. What matters here is not that I made that buttonhole but what I did with it. I took it on my first hard job interview when I went back to work and kept it with me for many years after that. I used to look at that buttonhole and say to myself, "If I can make a bound buttonhole in silk jersey, I can do anything, even this."

So you know those things you wish you could do? Do them. Sewing gives you this chance. Focus on that one fitting issue that makes you crazy and wrestle it to the ground. Do real quality every once in a while. Try that new finishing technique. See what you can do to make the inside as interesting as the outside. Leave your signature behind somewhere in each garment—your initials, a print rather than plain facing, or a decorative machine stitch as understitching on the wrong side of a collar. No one has to see it, but you will know, you will know.

Connect with the Community: Online and in Person

In the dedication to this book, I mentioned my grandmother's sewing group, the Sew 'n' Sews. Those ladies started meeting nearly a hundred years ago, in a particular time for that generation in that narrow window between the end of public school and when they were all due to disappear into marriages. What matters is that the Sew 'n' Sews kept meeting, and kept minutes, for the rest of their lives— well over 60 years. What the Sew 'n' Sews found when they sewed together endured.

These were my grandmother's best friends throughout her life. Well into her 90s, Grandma would identify someone in conversation as "one of the Sew 'n' Sews," members of her inner circle, those who had traveled with her through the Depression, a world war, empty nest, and two marriages.

Looking at a picture of the Sew 'n' Sews, I can't help but wonder what the group meant to these women, and the extent to which it represented a place to express creativity and ambition not possible in their day-to-day lives. It is interesting how naturally sewing, at heart a solitary activity, leads to social interaction.

When my children were little I used to go out in the evenings to teach sewing classes. I remember standing there in high heels, leaking breast milk, talking about how to insert zippers. I remember other young mothers arriving late and harassed without fabric or machines "just to sit here." I remember the woman who stayed after class one night to tell me in tears how her husband had retired and now expected a real lunch to be made, as well as an older woman who drove in from the country early and slept in her car until class.

But most of all, I remember those moments when a student went into the dressing room and came out with her garment done. I can see the top, dress, coat, or jacket, on over the jeans and sports-sock shoeless feet. I can see her turn around and I can still hear the comments, "You must be so proud of yourself," "You did a beautiful job," and most important, "No one will believe you made that yourself."

But they did and I was there. Now it's your turn.

The Sew 'n' Sews will be proud of you.

Sewspeak:
- -
Useful Terms and Tips
- -

The vocabulary of sewing requires some orientation. Different terms for the same process or materials are used in dressmaking and tailoring, and in home sewing and industrial garment manufacture. Here is my list of some common, and a few less common, sewing terms you may run across and my interpretation of what they all mean.

Alteration   An adjustment to a finished garment, usually to improve fit. Raising or lowering hems and taking in or letting out seams are all alteration activities. For some reason, style experts have started to refer to alteration as *tailoring*, which annoys me and must make generations of Savile Row tailors spin in their graves.

Apex   Used most often in pattern drafting as shorthand for the high point of the bust. Also known as the *nipple*.

Appliqué   This just means anything that is sewn to the surface of a fabric, but these days usually refers to decorative motifs that are applied by hand or machine.

Armo   A traditional name for the hair canvas interfacing used in serious tailoring of coats and suits. Use any currently available sew-in hair canvas when this is referred to.

Armscye   Dressmaker speak for an armhole

Atelier   A sewing workroom. An *atelier tailleur* is a couture workroom where suits and other tailored garments are made. An *atelier flou* produces dresses and other lighter women's wear.

Backstitch, hand   This is the strongest hand stitch you can make. Use a single or, for more strength, a doubled thread. (1) Bring the needle up through the fabric. (2) Instead of moving forward with the in and out of a running stitch, take a stitch back behind where the needle has come up, down into the fabric. (3) Bring the needle up one stitch length to the left of Step 1. (4) In each subsequent stitch, take a stitch backward to meet the previous stitch. From the right side, a backstitch will look very similar to a row of machine stitches. From the wrong side it will look like a series of double stitches.

Backstitch, machine   At the machine, a backstitch has a totally different meaning, referring to the few stitches forward and few stitches back. We all do this at the beginning and end of every seam to secure it. Taking a few stitches in place with the machine set at zero stitch length accomplishes the same end.

Ballpoint needles or pins   Most needles and pins operate on the pointy principle—they pierce the fabric because they are so sharp. However, even sharp points can still have difficulty puncturing some dense synthetic fabrics or knits. For either of these—a pin or needle—with a rounded point, hence a *ballpoint*, will move more easily through the fabric because it can spread the fibers. Ballpoint needles are easy to find; ballpoint pins are less so.

Bar tack   These can be made by hand, but most of us make bar tacks at the machine. Use them for extra security at the end of high action seams, such as at the top of pocket stitching or the bottom of a top-stitched fly. Some machines have a bar tack preprogrammed as a stitch. Otherwise, bar tacks can be made with a fairly wide zigzag stitch and a small stitch length, essentially a satin stitch. Remember to tie off each end of a bar tack made this way with a few straight stitches made at a zero stitch length.

Basting stitch, hand   Hand-basting stitches have an infinite number of uses in sewing. Primarily, they are used to hold tricky seams in place instead of pins, which are sometimes too wobbly. A seam in velvet should always be hand basted rather than pinned, for example. Basting can also be used to position patch pockets or other details in place before topstitching, or to hold down an edge, such as a wool collar before it is pressed. Try to use a different color thread to hand baste so it will be easy to see when it has to be removed. Silk thread is an excellent basting thread (save it for reuse after you use it) as this thread can be pressed over without leaving any indentations in the fabric. Basting stitches are usually fairly loose and long, about ½″ of stitch and then ½″ of space, made in and out with a longer needle for speed.

Basting stitch, machine   Machine "basting" is really just straight stitches made at the maximum stitch length possible on your machine. Machine basting is used most often for making parallel rows of gathering stitches, as in a sleeve cap where the fabric needs to be gently eased into a space.

Bat-wing sleeve   There are many variations of cut-on sleeves and among these bat-wing sleeves, sort of an exaggerated dolman, are the most extreme. A true bat-wing extends from the wrist almost to the waist.

Bespoke   In English tailoring, this is a term for garments made from custom-drafted patterns. This often indicates a client relationship where, once the patterns have been made to measure, the client can order garments to be made as required. I find it uncomfortable when bespoke is used to refer to any less serious endeavor.

Bias   Woven fabrics have three "grains"—lengthwise, crosswise, and bias. True bias runs diagonally across the fabric at a 45° angle. The chief characteristic of bias is its malleability and stretchiness. As a result, bias can be somewhat unstable, so it can be tricky along seams if not stabilized in the seam area in some way, but it drapes beautifully. Bias strips make excellent binding for curved edges as it can be pressed into shape before it is applied, and as a result can be sewn on without wrinkles. Bias-cut fabrics behave very much like knits in that they do not fray along the edges. It is not necessary to finish bias seam allowances, for example. Needless to say, garments cut on the bias require far more fabric then those that can be laid out orderly along the straight of grain.

Binding   A bound edge is any edge that has had the seam allowance removed and is wrapped with narrow strips of fabric to finish. Bias binding is used in most clothing as the edges bound in garments are curved-necklines and armholes, for example.

Straight-grain binding is fine when the edge to be finished is also straight. Bindings can be folded right sides together, stitched to the front of the item, and then turned to the wrong side where they are most often hand stitched in place; or sewn right side to the wrong side of the garment and then flipped to the right side, raw edge turned under, and topstitched in place. Make your own bindings; never use the purchased stuff, as the fabric quality is often poor.

Blind hem, machine   Most machines have some sort of machine blind hem stitch—you will recognize it by a series of straight stitches interrupted by a long and wide zigzag stitch—and a blind hem accessory foot. To make a blind hem by machine, fold up the hem allowance and then fold it back on itself so that only ¼″ or so of the cut edge of the hem allowance extends. Next start stitching with the straight stitches situated along the hem allowance and the zigzag swinging into the hem fold so it just nicks the fold a tiny bit. When the hem is smoothed down, only a tiny vertical hemming stitch should show on the right side. I use machine blind hemming, which makes a very durable hem, only in knit fabrics with some texture to further disguise the hemming stitches.

Bodice   This describes the body part of any garment between the waist and neck, excluding the sleeves and collar.

Bolero   A very short jacket, usually ending just below the bust, often with short or three-quarter sleeves. A bolero is an ancestor of the shrug.

Boning   Thankfully now made of rigid plastic rather than whale ribs. Boning is highly useful in making fitted garments, such as corsets, or to hold up strapless tops and dresses. Always applied in casings, usually in the linings or inside seam allowances that have been seamed together, boning can be added to the side and princess seams of any strapless dress for support. Just make sure you round off the ends of the boning so it doesn't poke through the casing.

Border print   Most often seen in cottons, border prints have one edge printed with a very dominant pattern, a row of flowers or geometric shapes, for example. Border prints can be very effective, such as when the border is laid along a hemline, but require much thought during the pattern layout stage and, of course, considerable extra fabric to work with.

Bound buttonholes   These are the classic buttonholes of fine dressmaker suits and slower to make than they are difficult. A typical bound buttonhole can be identified by the two fabric "lips" that fill the small faced opening.

Box pleat   Pleats are clever—designed to maintain the trim silhouette of a straight or A-line dress or skirt, yet still provide extra movement room where legs need it most. A box pleat is an inverted pleat centered behind the unstitched portion of a seam. Box pleats tend to be the largest of the pleats, generally one down the center front of a skirt or as a pair on either side of center front.

Breakpoint   Most often used in tailoring to describe the exact point where the front facing of a jacket or coat turns to the right side and becomes a lapel. To facilitate this turn, it is usual to clip through all seam allowances right to the stitching line at the breakpoint so the facing fabric can fold to the right side easily.

Bulk   This may seem like too obvious a term for a glossary, but it really matters. The phrase "eliminate bulk" is often used in sewing and often ignored. Captured by the keep-it-sturdy principle, many home sewists are reluctant to trim, terrified that somehow things will fray away. Trim anyway. Remember that bulk on the inside will always show on the outside, and who needs bumpy clothing? If you are worried about durability, double stitch over the seams where you might have to trim the most.

Bust   Breasts—as in bust measurements taken across a woman's chest right across the fullest part of her breasts.

Buttonhole twist   A heavier often slightly more finished kind of thread used tradition-ally to hand stitch buttonholes. It is now used most often for top stitching to add stitch definition or to sew on outerwear buttons. Note when using a thicker thread like this for top stitching, make sure you also use a machine top-stitching needle, the one with the large eye, so this thread can move easily during stitching.

Cap sleeve   A very short sleeve, some-times cut on and sometimes attached, with an underarm seam of only 1″–3″.

Casing   A fabric channel made by either folding over a top edge, as in the case of an elastic waist skirt, or an applied strip of fabric stitched to a lining, as in the case of a boned bodice. Casings are made to hold either elastic, a drawstring, or a supportive material such as boning.

Catch stitch   An X-shaped hand stitch sewn from left to right. Catch stitches are flexible and have some movement, so they are an excellent choice any time a pattern tells you to "tack down" a detail—a facing to a shoulder seam, for example, as these stitches will not pull or pucker. (For instruc-tions on making a catch stitch, see page 202.)

Center-slot zipper   Once used in most dresses, these are now used mainly in front zipping jackets or for decorative effect in some zippered pockets. Invisible zippers have made these less popular than they once were. Since the top stitching on both sides of the zipper needs to be evenly spaced in a centered zipper, I generally lay a piece of clear tape centered over the seam as a stitching guide when I have apply a zipper this way.

Chanel trim   The distinctive braid trim, sometimes simple, often elaborate, charac-terizes the classic collarless Chanel jacket. In knit sewing, the term is often used to describe any narrow, turned, and stitched knit trim around a neckline, armhole, or down the front of a closureless jacket.

Channel stitching   A form of garment quilting done through all layers—fashion fabric, lining, and sometimes a batting—to bond them all together. Tweed Chanel jackets are often channel stitched by hand or machine to hold the tweed, an underlin-ing, and a lining together. Close channel stitching also stiffens the fabric and so is also used frequently in accessories such as hat brims, belts, and bags to add structure to the fabric.

Chinese ball buttons   These are a great DIY substitute for hard buttons in any garment that buttons at the back. Made simply of narrow turned fabric tubes, these are essentially just a fancy sailor's knot. A lot of how-tos online. Fun to make.

Clapper   A smooth piece of hardwood that can be pressed hard down on any fabric that has just been pressed, to flatten and get a really sharp press. To increase the potency of the clapper, you can also lay the fabric down on a board and hit it hard—hence the name. Walk by any European tailor and you are likely to hear the noise of clappers at work.

Clean finish   This instruction, frequently given in reference to long edges like the facings, simply means to finish the raw edge so it won't fray but with minimum bulk. The most common options for clean finishing are serging the edge, turning it under once and topstitching, or binding it.

Clip   A small cut through the seam allowances, stopping just short of the stitching line, usually indicated in situations in which the fabric needs to be freed up to spread, as in around a curve or to turn at a point.

Closures   Not surprisingly, any device or notion used to close a garment. These would include buttons, zippers, snaps, hooks and eyes, and whatever creative solution you may come up with. Frequently also a design feature.

Continuous lap   A finish to the raw edges of the slit at the bottom of a sleeve above a cuff, often referred to in sewing patterns. These can be fiddly to do and can be bulky when complete, so I don't really like them at all and prefer instead to make a small tailored placket, like you would find in a

man's shirt, when I can. My advice: Look for a shirt pattern with this placket feature for sleeves with cuffs and save it to use in patterns that call for a continuous lap.

Convertible collar   You would recognize this as the typical camp shirt or bowling shirt flat collar—a collar without a stand that folds flat back onto a shirt or blouse to create a version of the notched collar. The convertible part of this collar comes from the fact that it can be worn two ways: buttoned to the neck or open with the facings turned back.

Corded buttonhole   A machine buttonhole with the satin stitch worked over a heavy thread—a buttonhole twist or even a pearl cotton—to add stability, polish, and density to the buttonhole. Most buttonhole feet have a hook at the back to hold the cording in place while the buttonhole is stitched. Corded buttonholes are beautiful on coats and jackets and make gap-proof buttonholes in knits.

Couture   In French, this simply means to sew, but many Anglos use the word to describe what the French call *haute couture* or high sewing. As the French mean it, haute couture is high-end, beautifully made, custom-fitted, custom-designed clothing. To the ordinary eye, this level of couture can be recognized by its exquisite fabrics, lovely details, and extensive use of hand stitching both in construction and in finishing.

Cross grain   The grain in woven fabric that runs across the fabric and perpendicular to the selvage edge.

Crotch point   The point at which crotch seams and inseams meet in a pair of pants.

Differential feed   In sergers/overlockers with this feature, the feed dogs come in sets, one behind the other under the foot. The differential dial moves the speed (and therefore the size of the steps) of the front feed dogs independently to those behind. A differential feed set to a higher number will increase the relative speed of the front feed dogs, easing in slightly more fabric to the rear feed dogs—counteracting the waving out that can occur in some knits, for example. When set to a lower number, the front feed dogs move more slowly, flattening out the puckering that can happen when serging fine or closely woven fabrics. A useful feature to have in any serger.

Dart   Darts are the mainstay of shaping fabric to fit over the contours of the body. Basically the job of a dart is to take in fabric where the body doesn't need it and to let it out where it does. An effective dart points directly at the high point or any body contour, and stops just short of it, ½″–1″ away. If your darts don't do these two things, or if they seem to take in too little or too much fabric, they will need to be adjusted (see Chapter 5: Altering a Flat Pattern to Fit, page 84).

Dart legs   The long sides, also the stitching lines, of a dart. The end point of the dart, where the stitching stops, is called the dart point.

Dauber   A tool used to apply extra moisture to very specific areas that need extra attention in steam pressing. This sounds more official than it is. Most work rooms use a bowl of water and a folded cloth or a device that looks like a giant cotton swab to daub a little bit of water here and there to details during pressing.

Degree of stretch   This is usually expressed in percentages and helps you identify the suitability of any fabric to a pattern designed for a particular stretchiness to achieve fit and comfort. (To help you determine degree of stretch, see the graphic, page 120.)

Delta   A term that home sewists once used to describe the pattern guide sheet. You still hear it used every now and then, particularly if you talk to my mother.

Direction of maximum stretch   It is really, really important you are able to identify this in a knit fabric. For comfort and fit, and to conform to the way knit patterns are drafted, the direction of greatest stretch needs to run across, not up and down, any pattern piece.

Dirndl   Think *The Sound of Music*. A dirndl is any skirt gathered at the top into a waistband.

Dolman sleeve   A garment style in which the bodice and sleeves are cut as one.

Dress form   Sometimes also called a *dress dummy.* These are useful fitting tools but only if they have been padded to reflect your own figure. Essential as well for designing clothes by draping fabric, if you don't have the luxury of working on live models like haute couture designers.

Dressmaker suit   A lovely term used to describe women's suits made by dressmakers, most often with distinctly more feminine lines than the counterpart manstyle suit. Fitted, interfaced button-to-the-neck jackets, often with Peter Pan collars and peplums, are typical of a dressmaker suit. Note these garments always, always had bound buttonholes, indicative of the craftsmanship and hand-sewing skills of the dressmaker.

Dressmaker's tracing paper   Not at all as used as it once was, this paper can still be a very useful marking tool. Similar to carbon paper (assuming you remember what that was) but waxed and frequently colored, tracing paper is laid wax side out between fabric layers. The sewist then uses a tracing wheel to run over important pattern details, which are transferred to the fabric in rows of tiny waxed dots. This method of marking is particularly useful for transferring patch pocket placement and for pleat and dart stitching and fold lines. Be aware that

once pressed, these markings can become permanent and in some fabrics show through. Always test before you use this method of marking.

Dropped sleeve   A sleeve in which the seam that attaches the sleeve to the bodice is dropped substantially from the end of the shoulder point, sometimes even a few inches down the arm. Most often seen in casual clothing.

Ease plus   A method for gathering up that bit of extra fabric necessary in some situations, such as easing in the top of a sleeve cap but without having to pull on gathering stitches. To ease plus, hold a flat finger behind the presser foot as you stitch, forcing the fabric to pack up behind the foot as much as you can. Inhibiting the exit of fabric out from under the feed dogs this way will make the feed dogs pick it up again slightly, creating the slight easing you need. I find I have to sew several lines of stitching this way to really get sufficient easing, but it works well in loosely woven wools and is faster than traditional gathering to ease.

Edge stitch   A kind of top stitch, always done from the right side, where the stitches are placed close to the edge of the fabric, generally ⅛˝ or so. Edge stitching is generally used to sharpen the edges of crisp fabrics such as gabardine or linen. For stitch definition, use a longer-than-construction stitch length.

Ensemble   Another term from the culture of women's dressmaking. An ensemble denotes a set of garments designed or specifically sewn to be worn together—such as a dress and matching coat or, more frequently, a matching top, skirt, and jacket—as opposed to a threesome of mix-and-match separates. More sophisticated than just an outfit. I would say the Queen nearly always wears some version of an ensemble.

Exposed zipper   My all-time favorite zipper to put in because, of course, it is the fastest. Usually reserved for outwear or bags, the exposed zipper is applied right side of zipper to the garment and stitched about ¼″ away from the zipper teeth, which are then exposed when the zipper is turned to the right side.

Face   As a noun, this is an industry term for the right side of the fabric. As a verb, it means to sew a backing to any detail.

Facing   A garment piece applied to an edge both to finish and support it.

Feed dogs   These are the little pointy teeth in a sewing machine throat plate that move the fabric along under the presser foot. You might be interested to know that stitch length is controlled by the feed dogs— big steps make big stitches and little steps make little stitches. Keep your feed dogs clean so they can make these moves easily.

Finger pressing   Smoothing a seam with your fingers in preparation for the next construction step or to crease it to make a temporary marking, as in fold in half to find a center point.

Flat-felled seam   A seam made by sewing wrong sides together, trimming one seam allowance down and folding the remaining longer seam allowance over and top stitching it down over that cut edge. A flat-felled seam is neat on both sides and is very strong. For this reason it is used in jeans construction and in shirts. (For information about an accessory foot that makes flat-felled seams very easy to sew, see Making a Flat-Felled Seam, page 162.)

Flounce   A kind of a ruffle made without gathering by cutting the fabric into a spiral within a circle. Much of a flounce is therefore cut on the bias, which makes it hang well.

French dart   Essentially two darts meeting at the middle with a point at each end, resembling a diamond. French darts are used when fabric needs to be taken in at the middle and then released into two body contours—a French dart in a bodice, for example, wider at the wearer's waist and releasing to the bust at one end and the hip or abdomen at the other.

French seam   A nice, neat seam, completely enclosed on the wrong side, suitable for lighter weight fabric. To make a French seam, sew the seam with a ¼″ seam allowance, wrong sides together. Press the seam flat and then turn and press again, right sides together. Next sew the seam again with a ⅜″ seam allowance and press.

French tack   Also known as a *swing tack*, a thread chain often made by several ½″ or so stitches between a lining and a garment so they can be attached but still move.

Gathering   To gather up a longer length of fabric to fit another, as in a gathered skirt or a gathered sleeve cap. Gathering is made by sewing in two to three rows of long machine basting stitches along the edge to be gathered (the more rows of gathering stitches, the more even the gathers) or by zigzagging over a length of heavier thread or cording. To make the gathers, pull along the bobbin threads of the machine basting, or if using the zigzag method (page 225), pull along the cord.

Gore   Vertical skirt panels, generally slightly A-lined or flared, as in a four-gore skirt, a six-gore skirt, and so on.

Gorge line   The seam that attaches the collar to the lapel/facing piece.

Grade   To trim two seam allowances but trimming one of these slightly more than the other to blend away right side show through of seam allowance bulk. Note that the seam will always have tendency to roll slightly to or "favor" the shorter, trimmed side. For this reason, the longer seam allowance is always the one closest to the right outward facing side of the garment.

Grain   A line in the fabric that can be drawn *directly* over the lengthwise or crosswise fibers that create the fabric.

Grainlines   Long lines, usually with arrows at each end, printed on patterns to help you lay the pieces so that they can be laid to measure an equal distance from the selvage.

Grosgrain   A kind of stiff ribbon distinguished by dominant vertical ribs. Because grosgrain does not bend easily, it is often used for support in dressmaking, such as to make waist stays (page 249), to face the button and buttonhole areas of knit cardigans, or to face waistlines and waistbands.

Gusset   A triangular or more often diamond-shaped insert added to areas where extra ease is needed for movement in tightly fitted garments. Gussets are typically added to under-arm seams or even to pants and leggings at the crotch point. The beauty of a gusset is that it adds so much wearer mobility but usually remains hidden in the lines of the garment.

Hair canvas   A heavy but pliable interfacing with a canvaslike appearance, sometimes with the little hairs that denote its classic fabrication from goat hair. Used extensively in traditional suit and coat tailoring, this interfacing is best when sewn in and can be shaped when necessary by hand stitches. Hair canvas provides a kind of substantial support without bulk to heavy fabrics that no other interfacing can match.

Ham   An indispensable pressing tool, and one that is shaped much like a real ham, that provides the variety of curved surfaces necessary for pressing anything but flat, straight seams. These come in the usual oval shape but can also be found with a variety of surfaces that are useful—my own has a kind of a nose on it that is good for small areas. Like all great pressing tools, a ham is covered on one side in cotton and the other in wool, to absorb different heats, and are always tightly packed with hardwood sawdust. Since wood captures and releases both heat and steam well, this assists in the actually pressing of the fabric as well as providing a shaping surface.

Hand   One of the most potent of all sewing terms and used throughout the industry to describe fabric quality and suitability for various uses. Hand literally means how does it feel in your hand. Fabrics are variously described as having a "crisp hand" or a "soft hand." The saying a fabric has a "good hand" is the ultimate fabric compliment, meaning it will sew well and produce a quality garment.

High bust   An accurate measurement that can capture true upper body size more accurately than the traditional bust measurement. (For more details on measuring, see What to Measure, How to Do It, and Why, page 66.)

Hong Kong finish   A seam-allowance seam finish in which raw edges are wrapped with binding. Cut the binding on the bias and it will not be necessary to turn the raw edges under on the underside of the binding, as bias does not fray.

Horsehair braid   Not surprisingly, this is no longer made of real horsehair. A stiff clear to white tape, "horsehair" is machine stitched to the bottom of full formal dress hems and then just flipped up and tacked to the seams. Once installed, the stiffness of the tape will hold a full skirt out and away from the body—an absolute necessity in bridal wear, for example.

Interfacing   A fabric that is attached by stitches or fusing to the wrong side of garment details for stiffness, support, or reinforcement. Use designated interfacing for best results, rather than trying to substitute with another layer of fabric. Typical areas that are always interfaced are collars, collar stands, cuffs, some button bands, and many hems (see The Backup Fabrics: Interfacing and Lining, page 131).

Interlining   Not to be confused with interfacing or underlining, interlining is a layer of special fabric added most often to outerwear as extra insulation or as a wind block to the garment. Interlinings are generally cut to match the garment piece to be interlined (often the back) and machine basted to it at the edges. I have interlined the body of fall jackets with cotton flannel, children's winter jackets with fleece, and the backs of coats with chamois leather.

Invisible zipper   Requires a special foot (get one from a dealer explicitly for your machine rather than the generic one from a fabric store) to install, although some folks do a great job with a regular zipper foot and using their fingers to spread the coils. Since there is zero topstitching in an invisible zipper, I think they are the easiest of all zippers to sew in and perfect for beginners (see instructions, page 164).

Keyhole buttonhole   These are the buttonholes with the little circle at one end. This circular opening accommodates a button with a shank and as such is the preferred buttonhole for outerwear of heavy fabrics that require those buttons.

Kick pleat   A short pleat in the back of a straight skirt to give you walking room. Usually these are small box pleats because they are a closed detail. A kick pleat covers the lining that might show when you walk, something that can happen with an open back skirt vent.

Kimono sleeve   A real kimono sleeve is actually a rectangle attached to a kimono, forming a boxlike sleeve. These kimono sleeves typically have a small opening in the seam under the arm for movement and enough room hanging in the corners of the sleeve to serve as sort of a built-in purse. In the West, however, a kimono sleeve often is used to describe any cut-on sleeve with an almost square angle under the arm.

Knife pleat   There are many descriptors for similar kinds of pleats—accordion, pinch, fan, and sunburst—but they all describe fine pleats. These may be pressed from waist to hem, sometimes in a circular skirt and sometimes vertically in the yardage before construction. These pleats are really difficult to make accurately yourself, but there are still pleaters in places like the New York garment district and online who will do the job quickly for you. Note that to pleat well and permanently, the fabric does need to have a high proportion of synthetic fiber in its makeup. Polyester is ideal.

Knot   Dressmakers traditionally knot hand-sewing threads by forming a loop around their index finger, rolling it off, and pulling on the thread to make a large knot. This was the first thing my mother showed me when I learned to sew at eight years old.

LBD   The "little black dress," the one garment all women are supposed to own and judging by office holiday parties, most of them do.

Magyar sleeve   Another, and apparently the Hungarian, version of the cut-on or dolman sleeve

Main   An industry shorthand term for main fabric (as opposed to lining, interfacing or contrast fabrics), often seen in cutting directions as in "Cut 2x main."

Memory   This describes the ability of a knit fabric or of an elastic to bounce back to its original dimensions after having been stretched. It is very important to assess memory in anything stretchy before you purchase. An elastic that won't snap back in the store is likely to get saggy pretty fast in a garment, and the same is true of any knit fabric that shows weak memory.

Muslin   It's a plain-woven fabric, a fit garment made from muslin, or an audition of a new pattern before it is made in the "good fabric."

Needle board   If you sew a lot of napped fabrics—velvet, for example—a needle board is quite useful. Essentially a mat with a metal pile, the needle board is used to support facedown napped fabrics. This allows them to be pressed from the wrong side without flattening.

Notch   A little triangular shape often seen along the cutting lines of patterns, used to match pieces during construction. I don't actually cut out these notches but make a little clip into the seam allowance anywhere they occur instead.

Notions   Sewist speak for all the stuff you need to make a garment, apart from the fabric, interfacing, and pattern. This includes threads, buttons, zippers, trims, and any other bits and pieces the garment might need.

Off-grain   Garment pieces or even entire garments themselves that are laid away from the marked grainlines.

Overlocker   The name for a serger in most places outside North America.

Pad stitching   Small diagonal hand stitches, more or less imperceptible from the right side of the fabric, used to attach a sew-in interfacing, such as hair canvas in tailoring. Pad stitching also is used to shape the piece—putting a roll in a collar, for example—and is often made while bending the fabric over your hand while it is worked.

Peter Pan collar   Nice, little, flat collars characterized by their curved shape. Most often seen in traditional little girls' dresses or in retro blouses and dresses. A lovely detail.

Petersham   Very similar to grosgrain ribbon, woven with one long edge somewhat shorter than the other so the ribbon curves in slightly. This makes petersham an ideal facing for skirt waistlines where it provides firm support and eliminates the need for the interfaced fabric facings.

PMIQ   Pin and mark in quarters. A shortcut measuring trick for dividing an opening into four equal parts. To PMIQ: (1) Fold the opening in half and put a pin at each fold. (2) Fold the opening in half again, but this time match the pins. (3) Put two more pins at the new folds. The opening will then have pins at each quarter point.

Point presser   A hardwood pressing tool (page 151) that I always describe as a Barbie doll ironing board. An essential tool for pressing open seams in hard-to-get-at areas, such as collars.

Princess seam   Essentially darts turned into seams, these are used to shape garments perhaps more smoothly than darts can. Princess seams run vertically in the garment and can start from the shoulder or the middle of the armhole. In either case they always run directly over the bust in the front and the shoulder blades in the back. Princess seams are wonderful fitting tools, particularly for curvier figures (see Chapter 5: Altering a Flat Pattern to Fit, page 84).

Raglan sleeve   Sleeves that connect with diagonal seams into the neckline rather than to the end of the shoulder.

RTW   Ready-to-wear. Clothing in standard sizes to be purchased "off-the-rack."

Revers   You sometimes see this term in the European sewing magazines. It means lapel.

Roll line   The line along which a collar or lapel folds back on itself. In tailoring, this line often is taped for definition and support.

Seam roll   A hardwood sawdust tightly stuffed fabric sausage (page 149) used to press open seams allowances without right-side indentation marks on the fabric.

Self   An industrial term often used in cutting to mean cut out of the same fabric as the main garment pieces.

Selvage   The finished, usually woven, edge running lengthwise along the length of the fabric.

Separating zipper   A zipper that opens at the bottom; used in outerwear.

Serger   The name for an overlocker within North America.

Set-in sleeve   A sleeve that is set into the bodice at the natural shoulder point, generally with an eased sleeve cap.

Shawl collar   A rolled collar without notches, made from an extended front and extended front facings, both seamed at center back. Classic bathrobes have shawl collars.

Sheath   A fitted one-piece dress, usually sleeveless and with a straight skirt.

Shirring   Gathering, usually in fine fabrics such as challis, lawn, or chiffon, and applied to specific areas of the body of the garment, such as shirring in a blouse below yoke.

Skipped stitches   A series of random long stitches that interrupt any line of machine stitching. Skipped stitches are almost always caused by using the wrong needle for the fabric. They can usually be eliminated by changing to a ballpoint needle for knits or even a leather needle depending on the fabric to be sewn.

Skirt marker   An old-school tool and a really useful one if you have no one around to help you pin up a skirt. Essentially a yard-stick set upright on a stand, the skirt marker allows you to mark a hem an even distance from the ground (the way all good hems should be marked). Some come with a puff of chalk to make the marks if you are work-ing on your own, and some have a lever that lets a helper line up pins to mark the hem. Definitely handy.

Slash   A scary-sounding way of saying cut right down the middle of something to open it up, as in slash open a welt pocket. The main thing to remember when follow-ing a slashing instruction is to cut right to the stitches with the slash—try putting a pin in the fabric as a barrier to make sure you do your slashing to and not through the stitching line.

Sleeve cap   The curved upper quarter or so of the top of a sleeve piece. In set-in sleeves, the sleeve cap is always eased in by at least two rows of machine-basting stitches. These are then pulled up slightly and steam pressed into shape until the sleeve fits smoothly into the armhole.

Sleeve head   A material stitched to the top of the armhole seam allowance and extending into the top of a tailored or formal wear sleeve cap. The purpose of the sleeve head is to support the cap so it won't collapse over the shoulder. In tailoring, a sleeve head may be a piece of fleece or lamb's wool. In puffy formal sleeves, the sleeve head can even be a tightly gathered tulle ruffle.

Slip basting   A kind of basting done from the right side of the garment, often to hold a detail in place in preparation for top-stitching. The lap side of a lapped zipper, for example, would be slip basted down before final stitching from the right side. Since holding things still is important in this kind of stitching, slip basting is usually done diagonally, almost like a loose whipstitch.

Sloper   Basic-fit garments with only minimal ease used as a foundation for understanding the fit of an individual figure. Slopers are too tight to be worn as garments. However, once they are used to establish fit, that information can be used to fit wearable garments precisely. Dress and pants sloper patterns can be custom drafted or purchased in standard sizes from the major pattern companies.

Stabilizers   Any material put under a fabric to help keep stitches, particularly embroidery stitches and buttonholes, flat and even. There are a wide variety of sta-bilizers available for purchase—cut-away, tear-away, and water soluble—and a few DIY ideas such as tissue paper, coffee filters, and printer paper.

Stash   Sewist slang for a fabric collection.

Stay stitch   Stitching done just inside the seam line prior to any construction to stabilize the grain of cut fabric edges, particularly those cut with a curve (see Stay Stitching, page 194).

Stay tape   A stabilizing tape applied anywhere that a specific edge needs to be kept from stretching. In tailoring, this may be a narrow twill tape hand stitched along a jacket roll line, around an armhole, or at the shoulder seams. In knit garments, this is usually a fusible tape or cut pieces of fusible interfacing pressed to shoulder seams or at the point of a V-neck.

Stitch-in-the-ditch   A way of securing a binding, facing, or other detail by machine stitching from the right side, aiming to put those machine stitches in the "ditch" or seamline.

Straight of grain   Refers to a pattern piece that has been laid so its center lies directly over the lengthwise fibers of the fabric. Laying out pattern pieces on the straight of grain is usually achieved by measuring from the selvage edge to each end of the marked straight-of-grain line printed on the pattern piece. When both ends of the line measure the same distance from the selvage, the pattern piece is lying straight of grain.

Stretch stitch   Often also called *reverse-action stitches*, because in most cases they are made by the feed dogs moving the fabric back and forth with every stitch. This movement essentially creates a strong double-stitched stitch that is meant to hold up under the seam stress of stretchy fabrics. In some cases, these stitches can be useful, such as when sewing crotch seams, that need to be very secure. In other cases, all that feed-dog action can stretch some knit fabrics out of shape. My best advice is to test each stitch on the fabric you want to use before you start a garment.

Tack   See catch stitch.

Take-up lever   This is the arm at the front of a sewing machine that moves up and down while you stitch. Of all the thread guides, the take-up lever is the most interesting as it actually measures out the length of thread necessary to meet the rotation of the bobbin. The take-up lever is always threaded after and not before the thread is nestled in the tension disks. In my experience, bird's nests—those awful messes of thread that can tangle up the lower part of the machine—are most often caused when the upper thread has bypassed or slipped out of the take-up lever.

Toile   In French, *toile de corps*, literally a fabric body, because it is just that—a close-fitting garment that mirrors the body with only minimal ease. Toiles are used to refine individual fit and not intended as wearable garments. An English term for the same thing is a *sloper*.

Two-way stretch   Knit fabrics that are stretchy both horizontally and vertically, most often required in active wear. Note that even when there are two ways the fabric stretches, it is still essential that the degree of maximum stretch be situated so it runs around the body, and the pattern laid out accordingly. If you have trouble determining the direction that stretches the most, pull on the fabric each way. The maximum stretch direction will have more bounce back. The direction of less stretch will return with less enthusiasm, a bit more like old bubble gum to my mind.

Tracing wheel   A spikey little wheel on a handle, used with dressmaker's tracing paper when marking a pattern.

Top stitching   Any stitching that can be seen from the right side and should therefore always be stitched from the right side.

Top-stitching thread   A heavier-weight thread used with a topstitch needle and a longer stitch length for well-defined stitching in heavier fabrics. If it is difficult to find a good color match of thread to fabric for topstitching, try using two construction threads in the needle, threading the two threads through the machine as if they were one.

Truing a seam   A fancy way of saying that if the seams don't quite match up properly after you have adjusted the pattern, just redraw them gently to blend until they do.

Turn of cloth   Understanding and respecting turn of cloth is one of the first principles of good sewing. Turn of cloth recognizes that fabric has volume. It understands that once stitched and turned, the internal bulk of seam allowances, even those that have been trimmed, can pull some other fabric edges in and shorten them. For example, turn of cloth explains why a pressed collar, in which the seams have been rolled under slightly to the wrong side, will no longer have even-cut edges, and the sewist should not try to force them to match, although she can trim them even (see Turn of Cloth, page 195).

Two-piece sleeve   A fitted sleeve design in which there is a second vertical sleeve seam running up near the elbow. Because a two-piece sleeve is able to follow the arm's shape more accurately than a one-piece sleeve, they typically have fewer wrinkles and hang more naturally. I always choose a two-piece sleeve pattern over a one-piece whenever I can, particularly when making jackets, coats, or long-sleeved woven dresses.

Two-way zipper   A zipper that can be opened from either the top or the bottom, easy to identify by the two zipper pulls. It is really important to use a two-way zipper in a coat or jacket—you are going to want to unzip just the bottom so you can sit down.

Under collar   Obviously the underside of a collar, but also a part of the collar that needs to be flexible and shouldn't peek out from under the top collar. Ideally a good under collar should be cut from its own pattern piece. These should be drafted to be slightly smaller than the upper collar and preferably cut in two pieces and seamed at the center. The reason for this center seam is that it will allow each under collar piece to be cut on the bias, keeping it supple.

Under stitching   An essential technique to prevent the wrong side of a facing, or similar detail, from rolling to the right side and showing. To under stitch, sew the seam, trim, grade, clip, and press. Then, stitch the seam allowance to the facing, placing the stitches as close as you can to the seam. Attaching the facing or under piece to the seam allowances will pull them slightly to the wrong side of the garment and keep them there.

Under lining   A layer of fabric attached by hand or machine stitches at the seam edges of the fashion fabric, intended to change that fabric's characteristics but substantially not its hand. A silk organza underlining, for example, is often added to a loosely woven fabric to add stability but not bulk.

Vent   An opening at the bottom of a garment made either for movement, as in the back vent of a straight skirt, or at the bottom of a sleeve before it is closed with a cuff.

Wadder   Any garment project that doesn't turn out as expected, as in you roll it into a ball and throw it across the room. We all have them; I certainly do.

Waist stay   A fabulous support around the waistline of very fitted dresses, often formal, to take the strain off the zipper. The stay is usually made of a sturdy grosgrain ribbon and is tacked to the inside of the garment at all seams at waist level except the center back. The ends of the stay are then closed with a hook and eye. When dressing, the waist stay is hooked closed and then the zipper zipped up.

Warp   The lengthwise fibers in a woven fabric.

Wearable muslin   A trial garment made usually to try out a new pattern or to fine-tune fit, but sewn in a fashion fabric rather than the traditional muslin. These are the experimental garments of optimists who hope they will get lucky and that their practice garments turn out to be entirely wearable.

Weft   Another term for woof (page 250).

Well of the seam   A term used to describe a seamline as seen from the outside of a garment. You will run across this in instructions that tell you to stitch-in-the-ditch a detail in place, "… laying the stitches directly in the well of the seam."

Welt pocket, single and double welt
Inset pockets in which the pocket bag is hidden behind the garment and accessed by a faced slot in the fabric. The welts, or lips, around the pocket opening can either be single or double. Welt pockets are most often seen in tailored jackets and coats and the back of pants. They are basically large, bound buttonholes with a pocket behind them. If you can make one you can make the other.

Whipstitch   The over and over stitch you probably already do but don't know what it is called. Whipstitching is most often used along a raw edge to finish. Couture garments frequently make use of beautiful, neat whip-stitch seam finishing.

With nap layout   Because so many fabrics have a definite shade difference running up or down the fabric—velvets, velveteen, corduroy, suede, and so on—it is important that the pattern pieces are all laid out in the same direction. Nap layouts require more fabric be purchased, too, which is why they have separate fabric requirements listed on the back of the pattern envelope. Sometimes nap layouts are also referred to as *directional layouts*.

Woof   The crosswise fibers in a woven fabric.

Yoke   A single pattern piece that covers the shoulders and attaches to both the front bodice or shirt front pattern piece and to the back. It provides a smooth and comfortable fit over the shoulders while leaving an opportunity for useful details in the garment body. For example, shirts often have a box pleat at the center back under the yoke to add extra shoulder-moving room, and many women's blouses have shirring under the front yoke to make room for a bust. Note that many skirt patterns also have fitted yokes, again providing a smooth fit over the hips and often releasing into pleats for movement.

Zigzag   The ability of a sewing machine to have a needle swing side to side in addition to just up and down when it makes a stitch. In addition to introducing a multitude of zigzag and even multi-directional stitches to home sewing, this function also means that machines that do a zigzag also have a wider needle hole in the throat plate. This wider hole can mean more jamming if you are not careful—the raw edge of the beginning of a seam can be pushed down into the machine when you start sewing (see Frustration 1: Fabric Jams, page 153).

Resources

- - - - - - - - - - -

Sewing Classics

It doesn't stop here at the end of this book; I am sure it's just a start. To help you on your way, I would like to share with you a short list of some of the best books ever written about sewing, all of which I still use and enjoy.

Don't be fooled by dates of publication of some of these resources. They are still widely available in public libraries and from online sellers. You will find many, many innovative ideas in these titles, supporting my contention that the 1960s to mid-1990s were the golden age of sewing books. During this period very smart women, many of them home economists, went deep into sewing and did terrific, thoughtful, original work. I sometimes wonder what careers such technically adept women would have had in another time, but then I think what a loss that would be to those of us who can still learn from them.

GENERAL SEWING

Bishop, Edna Bryte, and Marjorie Stotler Arch. *The Bishop Method of Clothing Construction*, Revised. Philadelphia, PA: J. B. Lippincott, 1966.

> Edna Bishop was a home-sewing forward scout responsible for some many of the best ideas in modern sewing. Pay close attention to the revelations on unit construction and fast details. Subsequent books by this team expanded further on specific garment types.

Hellyer, Barbara. *Sewing Magic!* La Grange, IL: Sew/Fit Co., 1979.

> The title really delivers. Hellyer is a genius and her techniques are magic. The focus is on smart, nifty ways to assemble tailored and knit shirts as well as vests.

Margolis, Adele P. *Fashion Sewing for Everyone*. Garden City, NY: Doubleday, 1974.

> Pretty much all of Margolis's books are gems, but this one goes right to common garment-making issues discussed with common sense, wisdom, and charm.

Zieman, Nancy. *10-20-30 Minutes to Sew*. Birmingham, AL: Oxmoor House, 1992.

> Nancy was a national treasure. Her books and past TV shows (*Sewing with Nancy*, available through nancysnotions.com) are wonderful places to launch a sewing self-education.

PRESSING

Taylor, June. *The June Tailor Method of Custom Detail Pressing*. Richfield, WI:
June Tailor, Inc., 1978.

> Pressing makes a huge difference in sewing, and it is so nice to have an authoritative
> reference that covers the subject in detail.

FITTING

Minott, Jan. *Fitting Commercial Patterns: The Minott Method*. Minneapolis, MN: Burgess
Publishing, 1978.

> This is an easy-to-understand fitting manual with straightforward block, slash, spread,
> and overlap techniques for making an infinite number of relevant flat pattern adjustments.

Oblander, Ruth, and Joan Anderson. *The Sew/Fit Manual: Making Patterns Fit: A Guide to
Pivoting and Sliding*. Bedford Park, IL: Sew/Fit Co., 1993.

> The original pivot-and-slide bible; extensive and original.

Rasband, Judith. *Fabulous Fit*. New York, NY: Fairchild Books, 1994

> Rasband went on to collaborate on more extensive fitting books, all worth reading for
> more information on the seam method, but this one, her initial work, is still very useful.
> Note that although Rasband talks about the seam method in the beginning of the book,
> she doesn't mention it consistently throughout the text. Look for the detailed illustrations
> on each fitting issue to see it being used.

Zieman, Nancy. *Pattern Fitting with Confidence*. Iola, OH: Krause Publications, 2008.

> Nancy was an early adopter of pivot-and-slide, and this is her simplified and clear guide
> to the method. Definitely a good place to start.

Garment Notes

When I chose garments to picture in this book, I was careful to use only what I considered everyday real-life clothes that reflected either a technique or a main idea discussed each chapter. My hope by doing this was that you would be encouraged to see patterns as tools, not merely as prescriptions for clothing, and yourself as someone who can wear exactly what you want because you sew.

CHAPTER 1
Why Sew?

Page 14: Cotton poplin shirt with bias-bound sleeve edge instead of hem. Cotton stretch twill pants.
PATTERNS: Style Arc Maggie shirt. Style Arc Margaret pants.

CHAPTER 2
What to Sew

Page 22: Dress, no closures, in rayon/polyester crepe; binding and decorative bow on shoulder in silk charmeuse; facings on armholes and on all hem edges replaced with bias binding.
PATTERN: Simplicity 8049 1960s-vintage three-armhole dress.

CHAPTER 3
Finding the Right Pattern

Page 36: T-shirt in rayon. Straight skirt in rayon/poly blend.
PATTERN: Jalie 3352 dolman top. Patternless skirt.

CHAPTER 4
If It Fits, They Will Wear It

Page 62: Tunic top in cotton broadcloth. Pants in stretch woven bengaline.
PATTERNS: Style Arc Blaire shirt. Style Arc Margaret pants.

CHAPTER 5

Altering a Flat Pattern to Fit

Page 86: Dress in prefused rayon crepe. Darts at back neck, darts at bust, and front seaming all provide more fitting opportunities than a standard, less-detailed, A-line shift dress. Neckline changed to wider V and dart end-points moved back 2″ toward side seams, shortening them for more modern and less articulated bust shape.
PATTERN: Simplicity 8254 1960s-vintage dress.

CHAPTER 6

Choosing and Cutting Fabric

Page 118: Dress in prewashed and dried linen. (For this chapter, I wanted fabric to speak for itself.)
PATTERN: Style Arc Autumn dress.

CHAPTER 7

The Gear Side of Sewing

Page 146: Shell (top with sleeves removed); lengthened 6″ and pivoted out 4″ at hem for more A-line shape; single-knit rayon blend with three-thread rolled hem, stretched while stitching for lettuce effect; shell fabric quite thin, so front is two layers, hemmed separately but attached to back at side seams and shoulders. Cardigan in rayon-blend sweater-knit. Pants in microsuede.
PATTERNS: Sewaholic 1201 Renfrew top. Jalie 3248 drop pocket cardigan.
Jalie 3243 pull-on pants.

CHAPTER 8

Mapping Out Your Own Sewing Strategy

Page 192: Knit cocoon dress; crossover V-neck treatment instead of pattern's faced neckline. Since pattern was drafted for woven fabric, I cut out dress a size smaller to allow for inherent ease in knit fabric.
PATTERN: Style Arc Adeline dress.

CHAPTER 9

Sewing for Joy

Page 228: Camp shirt in cotton; sleeves deep-hemmed and rolled up for more retro look; facing for waistline casing and pocket facings cut from shirt fabric as contrast. Shorts in chambray.
PATTERNS: Cutting Line Designs "Easy, Ageless, Cool" camp shirt. Jalie 3243 pull-on shorts.

About the Author

BARBARA EMODI sews, writes, and teaches in Halifax, Nova Scotia, Canada. She has taught sewing classes in Australia, Canada, the United States, and online, and has written extensively for a number of sewing magazines. She is also a past contributing editor of *Threads* and for many years wrote a monthly column for *Australian Stitches*.

Barbara sews everywhere she goes. Many of the samples for this book, in fact, were made in her travels, where she worked on picnic tables in campgrounds all over North America with the supervision and assistance of her extended family.

For more on Barbara, her sewing, and her ordinary life, visit her blog:

barbaraemodi.com

Photo by Karen Veinot

Want even more creative content?

Make it, snap it, share it *using* #ctpublishing